The Nine Year Plan
2022-2031
Messages of the Universal House of Justice

At Riḍván this year we described how, over the course of a quarter century, the Bahá'í world underwent a transformation that endowed it with an undreamed-of capacity to learn, to grow, and to serve humanity. But, however bright were the achievements of this period, they must be eclipsed by what is to come. By the conclusion of the new series of Plans recently begun, the Bahá'í community will need to have acquired capacities that can scarcely be glimpsed at present. In your deliberations over the coming days, you will be occupied with exploring what is required to bring into being such a fortified community.

-The Universal House of Justice

BAHÁ'Í
PUBLISHING
WILMETTE, ILLINOIS

Bahá'í Publishing
401 Greenleaf Avenue, Wilmette, Illinois 60091

Published 2022
Printed in the United States of America on acid-free paper ∞

25 24 23 22 4 3 2 1
ISBN 978-1-61851-215-4
Book design by Ethan Martin
Cover design by Patrick Falso
Cover photograph of entrance to the Seat of the Universal
House of Justice. Copyright © Bahá'í
International Community.

Contents

25 November 2020

To the Bahá'ís of the World

Dearly loved Friends,

We greet you with immense affection on this special 1.1
day, an occasion for calling to mind the power of the
Covenant, that power which "pulsateth in the body of the
contingent world" and forges enduring bonds of love among
the believers. In the months since Riḍván, we have seen the
evidences of this dynamic power in the unified activity
of Bahá'u'lláh's followers, led so ably by the institutions
of the Cause in each continent and country, as the
friends everywhere have sought with characteristic
creativity and determination to minister to the needs
of an ailing world. Your resilience and your unwavering
commitment to the well-being of those around you,
persistent through all difficulties, have filled us with
tremendous hope. But it is no wonder that, in some
other quarters, hope has become a depleted resource.
There is a mounting realization on the part of the world's
people that the decades ahead are set to bring with them
challenges among the most daunting that the human
family has ever had to face. The current global health crisis
is but one such challenge, the ultimate severity of whose
cost, both to lives and livelihoods, is yet unknown; your
efforts to succour and support one another as well
as your sisters and brothers in society at large will
certainly need to be sustained, and in places expanded.

1

1.2   It is against this background of furious storms lashing humanity that the ark of the Cause is about to embark upon a series of Plans that will carry it into the third century of the Bahá'í Era and significantly strengthen the Bahá'í community's capacity for realizing the society-building powers of the Faith. As you are aware, the first Plan to commence this new series will last but one year. In places where circumstances prevent national communities from establishing as many intensive programmes of growth before Riḍván 2021 as they intended, these twelve months will extend the time available to them to do so. Meanwhile, wherever the process of growth has already been intensified, the year will be an opportunity to consolidate the achievements made during the current Plan, while cultivating the conditions necessary for welcoming larger and larger numbers of souls into the embrace of a community recognized for its fortitude and outward-looking orientation. At the national, regional, and cluster levels, we look to communities of proven strength to help those in which less experience has accrued. In this year-long effort, every community must draw on whatever untapped potential it may possess and seek to overcome any obstacles that are impeding its growth, thereby preparing it for the demands to come. For it is within the context of a flourishing community, especially a centre of intense activity in a village or neighbourhood, and when each element of the Plan's framework is given the attention it requires, that those elements most visibly cohere and connect, multiplying the community's powers in the field of action.

Besides providing for advances within clusters 1.3
everywhere, the coming Plan will be a year for profound
reflection on the life of 'Abdu'l-Bahá and the strength of
the Covenant of which He was the Centre, as the community prepares to commemorate the centenary of His
Ascension. The observance of this anniversary will
undoubtedly prompt individuals and communities alike
to contemplate the significance of that infinitely poignant
moment when He Who was the Mystery of God
departed from this world. His passing took from the
Bahá'ís of that era a Figure Who was the object of their
ardent love and loyalty; to the faithful of this age, He
remains without parallel: a perfect embodiment in word
and deed of all that His Father taught, the One through
Whom the Covenant of Bahá'u'lláh was "proclaimed,
championed and vindicated". We are conscious that
the coming year will also mark a century since His Will
and Testament—that "momentous", "historic", "immortal"
Document—"called into being, outlined the features
and set in motion the processes" of the Administrative
Order, "the very pattern of that divine civilization which
the almighty Law of Bahá'u'lláh is designed to establish
upon earth". This "unique" and "divinely-conceived"
Order, this "mighty administrative structure", had been
fashioned by its Architect to perpetuate the Covenant
and channel the spiritual powers of the Cause. It will be
apparent, then, that the Day of the Covenant next year,
exactly twelve months from now, will be especially
meaningful. We ask National Spiritual Assemblies to
determine how these two dates, occurring so close
together, may each be observed, taking into account
prevailing conditions in their countries.

1.4   All the while, earnest preparations continue to be made in the Holy Land for the commemoration of the centenary of the Ascension of 'Abdu'l-Bahá at a gathering at which, it is hoped, representatives of National Spiritual Assemblies and Regional Bahá'í Councils will be present. Similarly, plans are already being made for the conference of the Continental Boards of Counsellors and Auxiliary Board members, which will coincide, in January 2022, with the lapse of one hundred years since the first public reading of the Will and Testament of the Master. Conditions in the world may, of course, require the plans being made for these gatherings at the Bahá'í World Centre to change. But come what may, we have no doubt that the efforts made in local communities worldwide to befittingly commemorate the Ascension of 'Abdu'l-Bahá and to honour the Day of the Covenant in this coming centennial year will provide the impetus needed to launch the succeeding stage in God's Minor Plan, even as Providence propels the unfoldment of His Major Plan in accordance with His incontestable decree.

1.5   The momentum that is sure to build with each successive cycle of the One Year Plan will be further augmented by the release of two films. The first of these, which will become available in time for the centennial commemoration, will be a portrait of the Person of 'Abdu'l-Bahá. Besides being a tribute to His life and work, it will explore how, by championing the oneness of humanity through His words and deeds, He offered a challenge to the stale assumptions and prejudices of the age, and gave stimulus to a process of unification which continues to this day. A second film, following soon after the first, will reflect on the expiration of the first hundred years of the Formative Age from the vantage point of the heights to which the Bahá'í community has climbed, and from where it can now gaze upon new horizons.

The significance of the occasions being marked during the One Year Plan will lend it a unique character, enhancing the work being undertaken in clusters and making this single year the ideal preparation for the global endeavour that is to follow. With a sense of joyful anticipation, we announce that the Bahá'í world will, at Riḍván 2022, begin a Nine Year Plan. Its requirements and provisions will be set out at a later date, but its duration already gives an unmistakable indication of the expansive prospect it will present. God willing, it will be heralded by the convocation of a series of conferences held over a span of months across the globe. 1.6

This, so far as it can be foreseen, is the course the Bahá'í community will seek to tread. For the present hour, we urge you to recommit your energies, keeping your focus on the mission immediately before you. We are immensely gratified to see the assured composure with which the community of the Greatest Name has sought to offer the divine remedy under all conditions, especially during this period when society's established patterns of life have been disrupted and risks of different kinds are being faced by so many. Withal, the friends must guard against being drawn into the ultimately futile conflict and strife that characterizes so much of the discussion of the affairs of society, or— 1.7

heaven forbid—allowing interaction of this type to permeate, even fleetingly, the conversations of the community. Yet such vigilance on your part in avoiding discord and in not becoming entangled in society's controversies should under no circumstances be construed as aloofness from the many pressing concerns of this time. Far from it. You are among the most active and earnest of humanity's well-wishers. But, whether through deeds or words, the merit of your every contribution to social well-being lies, first, in your resolute commitment to discover that precious point of unity where contrasting perspectives overlap and around which contending peoples can coalesce.

1.8   Less than two full cycles remain of the present Five Year Plan—indeed, of the current series of Plans inaugurated in 1996. In these closing months, we will be sure to offer ardent prayers on your behalf in our supplications at the Sacred Threshold. May you succeed in giving hope to those who know not where to find it in a world disoriented and adrift, sorely lacking the unity which you, through your heart-pledged devotion to the Covenant, so conspicuously manifest.

THE UNIVERSAL HOUSE OF JUSTICE

To the Bahá'ís of the World

Dearly loved Friends,

The final words in a most memorable chapter in the 2.1
history of the Cause have now been written, and the
page turns. This Riḍván marks the conclusion of an
extraordinary year, of a Five Year Plan, and of an entire
series of Plans that began in 1996. A new series of Plans
beckons, with what promises to be a momentous
twelve months serving as a prelude to a nine-year
effort due to commence next Riḍván. We see before us
a community that has rapidly gained strength and is
ready to take great strides forward. But there must be
no illusions about how much striving was required to
reach this point and how hard-won were the insights
acquired along the way: the lessons learned will shape
the community's future, and the account of how they
were learned sheds light on what is to come.

The decades leading up to 1996, rich with advances 2.2
and insights of their own, had left no doubt that large
numbers of people in many societies would be ready to
enter under the banner of the Faith. Yet, as encouraging
as instances of large-scale enrolment were, they did not
equate to a sustainable process of growth that could be
cultivated in diverse settings. Profound questions faced
the community which, at that time, it had insufficient
experience to answer adequately. How could efforts

aimed at its expansion proceed hand in hand with the process of consolidation and resolve the long-standing, seemingly intractable challenge of sustaining growth? How could individuals, institutions and communities be raised up that would be capable of translating Bahá'u'lláh's teachings into action? And how could those who were attracted to the teachings become protagonists in a global spiritual enterprise?

2.3   So it was that, a quarter of a century ago, a Bahá'í community that could still count three Hands of the Cause of God in its front ranks embarked on a Four Year Plan, distinguished from those that came before it by its focus on a single aim: a significant advance in the process of entry by troops. This aim came to define the series of Plans that followed. The community had already come to understand that this process was not just the entry into the Faith of sizeable groups, nor would it emerge spontaneously; it implied purposeful, systematic, accelerated expansion and consolidation. This work would require the informed participation of a great many souls, and in 1996, the Bahá'í world was summoned to take up the vast educational challenge this entailed. It was called to establish a network of training institutes focused on generating an increasing flow of individuals endowed with the necessary capacities to sustain the process of growth.

2.4   The friends set about this task aware that, notwithstanding their previous victories in the teaching field, plainly they had much to learn about which capacities to acquire and, crucially, how to acquire them. In many ways, the community would learn by doing, and the lessons it learned, once they had been distilled and refined by being applied in diverse settings over time, would eventually be incorporated into educational materials. It was recognized that certain activities were a natural response to the spiritual needs of a population. Study circles, children's classes, devotional meetings, and later junior youth groups stood out as being of central importance in this regard, and when woven together with related activities, the dynamics generated could give rise to a vibrant pattern of community life. And as the numbers participating in these core activities grew, a new dimension was added to their original purpose. They came to serve as portals through which youth, adults and whole families from the wider society could come into an encounter with the Revelation of Bahá'u'lláh. It was also becoming apparent how practical it was to consider strategies for the work of community building within the context of the "cluster": a geographic area of manageable size with distinct social and economic features. A capacity for preparing simple plans at the level of the cluster began to be cultivated, and out of such plans, programmes for the growth of the Faith arose, organized into what would become three-month cycles of activity. An important point of clarity emerged early on: the movement of individuals through a sequence of courses gives impetus to, and is perpetuated by, the movement of clusters along a continuum of development. This complementary relationship helped the friends everywhere to assess the dynamics of growth in their own surroundings and chart a path towards increased strength. As time went on, it proved fruitful to view what was occurring in a cluster both from the perspective of three educational imperatives—serving children, junior youth, and youth and adults—as well as from the perspective of the cycles of activity essential to the rhythm of growth. Part-way into a twenty-five-year endeavour, many of the most recognizable features of the growth process we see today were becoming well established.

2.5   As the efforts of the friends intensified, various principles, concepts and strategies of universal relevance to the growth process began to crystallize into a framework for action that could evolve to accommodate new elements. This framework proved fundamental to the release of tremendous vitality. It assisted the friends to channel their energies in ways that, experience had shown, were conducive to the growth of healthy communities. But a framework is not a formula. By taking into account the various elements of the framework when assessing the reality of a cluster, a locality, or simply a neighbourhood, a pattern of activity could be developed that drew on what the rest of the Bahá'í world was learning while still being a response to the particulars of that place. A dichotomy between rigid requirements on the one hand and limitless personal preferences on the other gave way to a more nuanced understanding of the variety of means by which individuals could support a process that, at its heart, was coherent and continually being refined as experience accumulated. Let there be no doubt about the advance represented by the emergence of this framework: the implications for harmonizing and unifying the endeavours of the entire Bahá'í world and propelling its onward march were of great consequence.

As one Plan succeeded another, and engagement 2.6 with the work of community building became more broadly based, advances at the level of culture became more pronounced. For instance, the importance of educating the younger generations became more widely appreciated, as did the extraordinary potential represented by junior youth in particular. Souls assisting and accompanying one another along a shared path, constantly widening the circle of mutual support, became the pattern to which all efforts aimed at developing capacity for service aspired. Even the interactions of the friends among themselves and with those around them underwent a change, as awareness was raised of the power of meaningful conversations to kindle and fan spiritual susceptibilities. And significantly, Bahá'í communities adopted an increasingly outward-looking orientation. Any soul responsive to the vision of the Faith could become an active participant—even a promoter and facilitator—of educational activities, meetings for worship and other elements of the community-building work; from among such souls, many would also declare their faith in Bahá'u'lláh. Thus, a conception of the process of entry by troops emerged that relied less on theories and assumptions and more on actual experience of how large numbers of people could find the Faith, become familiar with it, identify with its aims, join in its activities and deliberations, and in many cases embrace it. Indeed, as the institute process was strengthened in region after region, the number of individuals taking a share in the work of the Plan, extending even to those recently acquainted with the Faith, grew by leaps and bounds. But this was not being driven by a mere concern for numbers. A vision of personal and collective transformation occurring simultaneously, founded on study of the Word of God and an appreciation of each person's capacity to become a protagonist in a profound spiritual drama, had given rise to a sense of common endeavour.

2.7   One of the most striking and inspiring features of this twenty-five-year period has been the service rendered by Bahá'í youth, who with faith and valour have assumed their rightful place in the forefront of the community's efforts. As teachers of the Cause and educators of the young, as mobile tutors and homefront pioneers, as cluster coordinators and members of Bahá'í agencies, youth on five continents have arisen to serve their communities with devotion and sacrifice. The maturity they have demonstrated, in the discharge of duties upon which depends the advancement of the Divine Plan, is expressive of their spiritual vitality and their commitment to safeguarding humanity's future. In recognition of this increasingly evident maturity, we have decided that, immediately following this Riḍván, while the age at which a believer becomes eligible to serve on a Spiritual Assembly shall remain twenty-one, the age at which a believer may vote in Bahá'í elections shall be lowered to eighteen. We have no doubt that Bahá'í youth everywhere who are of age will vindicate our confidence in their ability to fulfil "conscientiously and diligently" the "sacred duty" to which every Bahá'í elector is called.

We are conscious that, naturally, the realities 2.8 of communities differ greatly. Different national communities, and different places within those communities, began this series of Plans at different points of development; since then, they have also developed at different speeds and have attained different levels of progress. This, in itself, is nothing new. It has always been the case that conditions in places vary, as does the degree of receptivity found there. But we perceive, too, a swelling tide, whereby the capacity, confidence and accumulated experience of most communities are rising, buoyed by the success of their sister communities near and far. As an example, while souls who arose to open a new locality in 1996 lacked nothing for courage, faith and devotion, today their counterparts everywhere combine those same qualities with knowledge, insights and skills that are the accumulation of twenty-five years of effort by the entire Bahá'í world to systematize and refine the work of expansion and consolidation.

Regardless of a community's starting point, it has 2.9 advanced the process of growth when it has combined qualities of faith, perseverance and commitment with a readiness to learn. In fact, a cherished legacy of this series of Plans is the widespread recognition that any effort to advance begins with an orientation towards learning. The simplicity of this precept belies the significance of the implications that follow from it. We do not doubt that every cluster, given time, will progress along the continuum of development; the communities that have advanced most quickly, relative to those whose circumstances and possibilities were similar, have shown an ability to foster unity of thought and to learn about effective action. And they did so without hesitating to act.

2.10 A commitment to learning also meant being prepared to make mistakes—and sometimes, of course, mistakes brought discomfort. Unsurprisingly, new methods and approaches were handled inexpertly at first because of a lack of experience; on occasion, a newly acquired capacity of one kind was lost as a community became absorbed in developing another. Having the best of intentions is no guarantee against making missteps, and moving past them requires both humility and detachment. When a community has remained determined to show forbearance and learn from mistakes that naturally occur, progress has never been out of reach.

2.11 Midway through the series of Plans, the community's involvement in the life of society began to become the focus of more direct attention. The believers were encouraged to think of this in terms of two interconnected areas of endeavour—social action and participation in the prevalent discourses of society. These, of course, were not alternatives to the work of expansion and consolidation, much less distractions from it: they were inherent within it. The greater the human resources a community could call on, the greater became its capacity to bring the wisdom contained in Bahá'u'lláh's Revelation to bear upon the challenges of the day—to translate His teachings into reality. And the troubled affairs of humankind over this period seemed to underline how desperate was its need for the remedy prescribed by the Divine Physician. Implied in all this was a conception of religion very different from those holding sway in the world at large: a conception which recognized religion as the potent force propelling an ever-advancing civilization. It was understood that such a civilization would also not appear spontaneously, of its own accord—it was the mission of Bahá'u'lláh's followers to labour for its emergence. Such a mission demanded applying the same process of systematic learning to the work of social action and engagement in public discourse.

Viewed from the perspective of the last two and a half decades, the capacity for undertaking social action has risen markedly, leading to an extraordinary efflorescence of activity. Compared with 1996, when some 250 social and economic development projects were being sustained from year to year, there are now 1,500, and the number of Bahá'í-inspired organizations has quadrupled to surpass 160. More than 70,000 grassroots social action initiatives of short duration are being undertaken each year, a fifty-fold increase. We look forward to a continued rise in all these endeavours resulting from the dedicated support and stimulus

2.12

15

now provided by the Bahá'í International Development Organization. Meanwhile, Bahá'í participation in the prevalent discourses of society has also grown immensely. Besides the many occasions when the friends find they can offer a Bahá'í perspective in conversations that occur in a work or personal context, more formal participation in discourses has significantly advanced. We have in mind not only the much-expanded efforts and increasingly sophisticated contributions of the Bahá'í International Community—which in this period added Offices in Africa, Asia and Europe—but also the work of a vastly augmented, greatly fortified network of national Offices of External Affairs, for whom this area of endeavour became the principal focus; in addition, there were insightful and notable contributions made by individual believers to specific fields. All this goes some way towards explaining the esteem, appreciation and admiration which leaders of thought and other prominent figures at all levels of society have again and again expressed for the Faith, its followers and their activities.

2.13   In reviewing the entire twenty-five-year period, we are awed by the many kinds of progress the Bahá'í world has made concurrently. Its intellectual life has thrived, as demonstrated not only by its advances in all the areas of endeavour already discussed, but also by the volume of high-quality literature published by Bahá'í authors, by the development of spaces for the exploration of certain disciplines in the light of the teachings, and by the impact of the undergraduate and graduate seminars systematically offered by the

Institute for Studies in Global Prosperity, which, in collaboration with the institutions of the Cause, now serves Bahá'í youth from well over 100 countries. Efforts to raise up Houses of Worship have very visibly accelerated. The last Mother Temple was erected in Santiago, Chile, and projects to build two national and five local Mashriqu'l-Adhkárs were initiated; the Houses of Worship in Battambang, Cambodia, and Norte del Cauca, Colombia, have already opened their doors. Bahá'í Temples, whether newly dedicated or long established, are increasingly occupying a position at the heart of community life. The material support offered by the rank and file of the believers for the myriad endeavours undertaken by the friends of God has been unstinting. Simply viewed as a measure of collective spiritual vitality, the generosity and sacrifice with which, at a time of considerable economic upheaval, the critical flow of funds has been maintained—nay, invigorated—is most telling. In the realm of Bahá'í administration, the capacity of National Spiritual Assemblies to manage the affairs of their communities in all their growing complexity has been considerably enhanced. They have benefited in particular from new heights of collaboration with the Counsellors, who have been instrumental in systematizing the gathering of insights from the grassroots across the world and ensuring they are widely disseminated. This was also the period in which the Regional Bahá'í Council emerged as a fully fledged institution of the Cause, and in 230 regions now, Councils and those training institutes they oversee have proved themselves indispensable for advancing the process of growth. To

17

extend into the future the functions of the Chief Trustee of Ḥuqúqu'lláh, the Hand of the Cause of God 'Alí-Muḥammad Varqá, the International Board of Trustees of Ḥuqúqu'lláh was established in 2005; today it coordinates the efforts of no less than 33 National and Regional Boards of Trustees that now compass the globe, which in turn guide the work of over 1,000 Representatives. The developments which occurred at the Bahá'í World Centre during this same period are many: witness the completion of the Terraces of the Shrine of the Báb and two buildings on the Arc and the commencement of the construction of the Shrine of 'Abdu'l-Bahá, not to mention a host of projects to strengthen and preserve the precious Holy Places of the Faith. The Shrine of Bahá'u'lláh and the Shrine of the Báb were recognized as World Heritage sites, places of inestimable significance for humanity. The public flocked to these sacred locations in their hundreds of thousands, approaching one and a half million in some years, and the World Centre regularly welcomed hundreds of pilgrims at once, sometimes more than 5,000 in a year, along with a similar number of Bahá'í visitors; we are delighted as much by the raised numbers as by the scores of different peoples and nations represented among those who partake of the bounty of pilgrimage. The translation, publication and dissemination of the Sacred Texts has also been greatly accelerated, in parallel with the development of the Bahá'í Reference Library, one of the most notable members of the growing family of websites associated with Bahai.org, which itself is now available in ten languages. A variety of offices and agencies have been established, situated at the World Centre and elsewhere, charged with supporting the process of learning unfolding across multiple areas of endeavour throughout the Bahá'í world. All this, our sisters and brothers in faith, is but a fraction of the tale we could recount of what your devotion to Him Who was the Wronged One of the World has brought forth. We can but echo the poignant words once voiced by the beloved Master when, overcome with emotion, He cried out: "O Bahá'u'lláh! What hast Thou done?"

*

From the panorama of a pivotal quarter century, 2.14 we now direct our focus to the most recent Five Year Plan, a Plan quite unlike any that has gone before in a variety of ways. In this Plan we urged the Bahá'ís of the world to draw on all that they had learned in the previous twenty years and put it to full effect. We are delighted that our hopes in this regard were more than met, but while we would naturally expect great things from the followers of the Blessed Beauty, the character of what was achieved through their herculean efforts was truly breathtaking. It was the capstone to an accomplishment twenty-five years in the making.

The Plan was especially memorable for being trisected 2.15 by two sacred bicentenaries, each of which galvanized local communities the world over. The company of the faithful demonstrated, on a scale never previously witnessed and with relative ease, a capacity to engage people from all sections of society in honouring the life

19

of a Manifestation of God. It was a powerful indicator of something broader: the ability to channel the release of tremendous spiritual energies for the advancement of the Cause. So magnificent was the response that in many places the Faith was propelled out of obscurity at the national level. In settings where it was unexpected, perhaps unlooked for, marked receptivity to the Faith became apparent. Thousands upon thousands upon thousands were transported by their encounter with a devotional spirit that is today characteristic of Bahá'í communities everywhere. The vision of what is made possible by observing a Bahá'í Holy Day was immeasurably expanded.

2.16 The achievements of the Plan, simply in numerical terms, quickly eclipsed those of all the Plans that had preceded it since 1996. At the start of this Plan, the capacity existed for conducting just over 100,000 core activities at a given time, a capacity that was the fruit of twenty years of common endeavour. Now, 300,000 core activities are being sustained at once. Participation in those activities has risen above two million, which is also close to a threefold increase. There are 329 national and regional training institutes in operation, and their capacity is evidenced by the fact that three-quarters of a million people have been enabled to complete at least one book of the sequence; overall, the number of courses completed by individuals is now also two million—a rise of well over a third in five years.

2.17 The increased intensity with which programmes of growth around the world are being pursued tells an impressive story of its own. In this five-year span, we had called for growth to be accelerated in every one of the 5,000 clusters where it had begun. This imperative became the impetus for earnest endeavour throughout the world. As a result, the number of intensive programmes of growth more than doubled and now stands at approximately 4,000. Difficulties involved in opening up new villages and neighbourhoods to the Faith in the midst of a global health crisis, or expanding activities that were at an early stage when the pandemic began, prevented an even higher total from being reached during the Plan's final year. However, there is more to tell than this. At the outset of the Plan, we had expressed the hope that the number of clusters where the friends had passed the third milestone along a continuum of growth, as a consequence of learning how to welcome large numbers into the embrace of their activities, would grow by hundreds more. That total then stood at around 200, spread across some 40 countries. Five years on, this number has risen to an astonishing 1,000 in nearly 100 countries—a quarter of all the intensive programmes of growth in the world and an achievement far surpassing our expectations. And yet even these figures do not reveal the loftiest heights to which the community has soared. There are over 30 clusters where the number of core activities being sustained exceeds 1,000; in places, the total is several thousand, involving the participation of more than 20,000 people in a single cluster. A growing number of Local Spiritual Assemblies now oversee the unfoldment of educational programmes that cater to practically all the children and junior youth in a village; the same reality is beginning to emerge within a few urban neighbourhoods. Engagement with the Revelation of Bahá'u'lláh has, in notable instances, transcended individuals, families and extended kinships—what is being witnessed is the movement of populations towards a common centre. At times, age-old hostilities between opposing groups are being left behind, and certain social structures and dynamics are being transformed in the light of the divine teachings.

2.18   We cannot but be overjoyed at advances so impressive. The society-building power of the Faith of Bahá'u'lláh is being manifested with ever more clarity, and this is a firm foundation upon which the coming Nine Year Plan will build. Clusters of marked strength, as had been hoped, have proven to be reservoirs of knowledge and resources for their neighbours. And regions where more than one such cluster exist have more easily developed the means to accelerate growth in cluster after cluster. We feel compelled to stress again, however, that progress has been near universal; the difference in progress between one place and another is of degree. The community's collective understanding of the process of entry by troops and its confidence in being able to stimulate this process under any set of circumstances have risen to levels that were unimaginable in decades past. The profound questions that had loomed for so long, and which were brought into sharp focus in 1996, have been convincingly answered by the Bahá'í world. There is a generation of believers whose entire lives bear the imprint of the community's progress. But the sheer scale of what has occurred in those many clusters where the frontiers of learning are being extended has turned a significant advance in the process of entry by troops into a momentous one of historic proportions.

Many will be familiar with how the Guardian 2.19 divided the Ages of the Faith into consecutive epochs; the fifth epoch of the Formative Age began in 2001. Less well known is that the Guardian also made specific reference to there being epochs of the Divine Plan, and stages within those epochs. Held in abeyance for two decades while local and national organs of the Administrative Order were being raised up and strengthened, the Divine Plan conceived by 'Abdu'l-Bahá was formally inaugurated in 1937 with the commencement of the first stage of its first epoch: the Seven Year Plan assigned by the Guardian to the North American Bahá'í community. This first epoch closed after the conclusion of the Ten Year Crusade in 1963, which had resulted in the banner of the Faith being planted across the world. The opening stage of the second epoch was the first Nine Year Plan, and no less than ten Plans have followed in its wake, Plans that have ranged in duration from twelve months to seven years. At the dawn of this second epoch, the Bahá'í world was already witnessing the earliest beginnings of that entry into the Faith by troops that had been foreseen by the Author of the Divine Plan; in the succeeding decades, generations of devoted believers within the community of the Greatest Name have laboured in the Divine Vineyard to cultivate the

23

conditions required for sustained, large-scale growth. And at this glorious season of Riḍván, how abundant are the fruits of those labours! The phenomenon of sizeable numbers swelling the activities of the community, catching the spark of faith and swiftly arising to serve at the leading edge of the Plan has moved from being a forecast sustained by faith to a recurring reality. Such a pronounced and demonstrable advance demands to be marked in the annals of the Cause. With elated hearts, we announce that the third epoch of the Master's Divine Plan has begun. Stage by stage, epoch after epoch shall His Plan unfold, until the light of the Kingdom illumines every heart.

*

2.20   Beloved friends, no review of the five-year enterprise that concluded the second epoch of the Divine Plan would be complete without special reference to the upheavals that accompanied its final year and which persist still. The restrictions on personal interaction that waxed and waned in most countries over this period could have dealt the community's collective efforts a severe blow, recovery from which might have taken years, but there are two reasons why this was not the case. One was the widespread consciousness of the duty of Bahá'ís to serve humanity, never more so than in times of peril and adversity. The other was the extraordinary rise in capacity in the Bahá'í world to give expression to that consciousness. Accustomed over many years to adopting patterns of systematic action, the friends brought their creativity and sense of purpose to bear on an unforeseen crisis, while ensuring that the new approaches they developed were coherent with the framework they had laboured in successive Plans to perfect. This is not to overlook the serious hardships being endured by Bahá'ís, like their compatriots in every land; yet throughout severe difficulties, the believers have remained focused. Resources have been channelled to communities in need, elections went ahead wherever possible, and in all circumstances the institutions of the Cause have continued to discharge their duties. There have even been bold steps forward. The National Spiritual Assembly of São Tomé and Príncipe will be re-established this Riḍván, and two new pillars of the Universal House of Justice will be raised up: the National Spiritual Assembly of Croatia, with its seat in Zagreb, and the National Spiritual Assembly of Timor-Leste, with its seat in Dili.

And so the One Year Plan begins. Its purpose and requirements have already been set out in our message sent on the Day of the Covenant; this Plan, though brief, will suffice to prepare the Bahá'í world for the Nine Year Plan that is to follow. A period of special potency, which opened one hundred years after the revelation of the Tablets of the Divine Plan, will soon close with the centenary of the Ascension of 'Abdu'l-Bahá, marking the conclusion of the first century of the Formative Age and the start of the second. The company of the faithful enter this new Plan at a time when humanity, chastened by the exposure of its vulnerability, seems more conscious of

2.21

the need for collaboration to address global challenges. Yet, lingering habits of contest, self-interest, prejudice and closed-mindedness continue to hinder the movement towards unity, despite growing numbers in society who are showing in words and deeds how they, too, yearn for greater acceptance of humanity's inherent oneness. We pray that the family of nations may succeed in putting aside its differences in the interests of the common good. Notwithstanding the uncertainties that shroud the months ahead entreat Bahá'u'lláh to make the confirmations that have sustained His followers for so long more abundant still, that you may be carried forward in your mission, your composure undisturbed by the turbulence of a world whose need for His healing message is ever more acute.

2.22   The Divine Plan enters a new epoch and a new stage. The page is turned.

THE UNIVERSAL HOUSE OF JUSTICE

25 November 2021

To the Friends Gathered in the Holy Land
to Mark the Centenary Commemoration
of the Ascension of 'Abdu'l-Bahá

Our hearts are filled with wonder as we contem- 3.1
plate the significance of this momentous occasion: the
close of one hundred years since the passing of
'Abdu'l-Bahá, one hundred years since the inception of
the Formative Age of the Bahá'í Dispensation, and one
hundred years since the Faith of Bahá'u'lláh was
entrusted to His Administrative Order, whose institutions you here represent. How marvellous is His
Covenant, through which "this unique, this wondrous
System" has been established in your nations and its
processes made to operate. We bow our heads in gratitude to Bahá'u'lláh that, despite the numerous and
severe obstacles of a world in turmoil, He has opened
the doors and facilitated the means for you—including, for the first time, representatives of Regional Bahá'í
Councils—to be here during these soul-stirring days.

A period of special potency which began in 2016 3.2
with the centenary of the revelation of the Tablets
of the Divine Plan and included the bicentennial
anniversaries of the Birth of the Twin Manifestations of
God is now, a hundred years after 'Abdu'l-Bahá's
passing, drawing to a close. The advancements the
Bahá'í community has made during this time have

been nothing less than extraordinary. These have prepared the believers everywhere to meet the demands and fulfil the requirements of the next stage of 'Abdu'l-Bahá's Divine Plan, which is to commence just months from now and will last nine years. The accelerating decline of the current social order, and the growing need for constructive processes that will lead to the emergence of a new world society, are daily more evident. A century after the Master bequeathed to the followers of the Greatest Name a document which contains priceless elements for building a divine civilization, we are reminded of the words of the beloved Guardian: "The champion builders of Bahá'u'lláh's rising World Order must scale nobler heights of heroism as humanity plunges into greater depths of despair, degradation, dissension and distress."

3.3   Beloved friends, on this Day of the Covenant we all look to its Centre and recall the life and Person of 'Abdu'l-Bahá, a Figure Whose very being was the embodiment of the Covenant, that pivotal centre of unity for all humankind, binding together the multitudinous peoples of the earth. 'Abdu'l-Bahá, that Mystery of God, "a sign of His greatness", and "the most perfect bounty", Who is treasured in the pure hearts of countless children, youth, and adults, is surely watching over and aiding His loved ones, ever casting His eye of protection over them. In these uncertain times, the friends turn with hope and longing to 'Abdu'l-Bahá, that "shelter for all mankind", "a shield unto all who are in heaven and on earth", beseeching His assistance from the realms above as they endeavour to follow His example in the path of service. During the coming days, when the thoughts of the believers all around the world are focused on "this sacred and glorious Being", you have the blessing and privilege of paying homage to Him on behalf of your communities in those very spots where He laboured day and night for the promotion of the Cause of God and for the betterment of humankind.

Tomorrow night, on the eve of the centenary of His 3.4 passing, we will hold His loved ones throughout the world in our hearts as we pray in the sacred room where the final moments of His earthly life were spent. We will ardently supplicate that the healing message for which 'Abdu'l-Bahá lived and sacrificed His all may, before long, find a home in the hearts and souls of all humanity and that the efforts of the friends of God to this end may be acceptable in His sight.

THE UNIVERSAL HOUSE OF JUSTICE

ON THE OCCASION OF THE CENTENARY COMMEMORATION OF THE ASCENSION OF 'ABDU'L-BAHÁ

A Tribute by the Universal House of Justice

A century has now elapsed since the noble spirit of 'Abdu'l-Bahá ascended to its eternal home. His birth had coincided with the dawn of the Faith's Heroic Age, and His passing signalled the setting of the sun upon its final epoch. No clearer demonstration could be imagined of how He embodied the forces of unity than the sight of His funeral, at which a vast crowd of mourners from every creed in this land came together to grieve their common loss. In His day, so many of the friends who embraced the Faith absorbed the spirit of the divine teachings simply by observing Him; still today, if we wish to align our lives with that same spirit, we look to the example set by the Master, Whose word and deed reflected the brilliance of the light that shone from Bahá'u'lláh's Revelation. 4.1

In every respect, His example is central to Bahá'í identity. Every Bahá'í may turn to Him to understand better how to diffuse the light of the Faith and for a model to follow as we seek to awaken spiritual susceptibilities in those we encounter. His own counsel, that the teacher must be "fully enkindled" so that 4.2

his utterance may "exert influence", and yet be "totally self-effaced and evanescent" so that "he may teach with the melody of the Concourse on high", is vividly realized in the unnumbered accounts of souls transformed by being in the company of 'Abdu'l-Bahá. Countless are the lessons to be learned from how He presented the divine precepts to every kind of person, constantly widening the circle of unity, without regard for any outward dissimilarities of appearance, language, custom, or belief. The universality of His love produced a community that, even at that time, could justly claim to be a cross-section of society. His love revived, nurtured, inspired; it banished estrangement and welcomed all to the banquet table of the Lord. Every community-building endeavour undertaken today, every educational activity and every outreach, carries with it the hope of communicating, through our own efforts, a token of the same love He showered upon every soul. Such efforts are the best tribute that can be rendered to Him, at this centenary and every day that follows.

4.3   We offer thanks to Bahá'u'lláh for having given the world not only, in His teachings, a standard of purity, devotion, and integrity to which souls may forever aspire, but also, in the Figure of the Master, a flawless example of how life can be lived to that standard. As humanity is beset by crisis after crisis, the community of the Greatest Name, which cannot avoid exposure to such upheavals, is privileged to have before it the model of 'Abdu'l-Bahá. Neither peril nor obstacle would prevent Him from discharging His mission, whether by attending to the needs of the hour or preparing for the future; neither hostility nor events of the world would divert Him from His course. Serene, confident, and resolute, He was unperturbed by setbacks, welcoming hardship and adversity in the path of God. How relentless were the attacks upon Him! How deplorable the burdens He had to bear! We recall the testimony of His distinguished sister, the Greatest Holy Leaf, that "in the dark of the night, out of the depths of His bosom, could be heard His burning sighs, and when the day broke, the wondrous music of His prayers would rise up to the denizens of the realm on high."

The passage of time has not diminished the awe   4.4
with which we regard "the rôle and character of One Who, not only in the Dispensation of Bahá'u'lláh but in the entire field of religious history, fulfils a unique function." And as Shoghi Effendi has further affirmed of Him:

He is, and should for all time be regarded, first   4.5
and foremost, as the Centre and Pivot of Bahá'u'lláh's peerless and all-enfolding Covenant, His most exalted handiwork, the stainless Mirror of His light, the perfect Exemplar of His teachings, the unerring Interpreter of His Word, the embodiment of every Bahá'í ideal, the incarnation of every Bahá'í virtue, the Most Mighty Branch sprung from the Ancient Root, the Limb of the Law of God, the Being "round Whom all names revolve", the Mainspring of the Oneness of Humanity, the Ensign of the Most Great Peace, the

Moon of the Central Orb of this most holy Dispensation—styles and titles that are implicit and find their truest, their highest and fairest expression in the magic name 'Abdu'l-Bahá. He is, above and beyond these appellations, the "Mystery of God"—an expression by which Bahá'u'lláh Himself has chosen to designate Him, and which, while it does not by any means justify us to assign to Him the station of Prophethood, indicates how in the person of 'Abdu'l-Bahá the incompatible characteristics of a human nature and superhuman knowledge and perfection have been blended and are completely harmonized.

4.6   Dearest co-workers: We summoned you here not only to honour the memory of 'Abdu'l-Bahá and to recall His trials and triumphs, but also, with us, to rededicate yourselves and the communities you represent to earnestly serving the Cause to which He devoted His very existence. In fulfilment of the sacred charge laid upon Him by the Blessed Beauty, He gave the Bahá'í world custody of two Charters that have guided its progress and development ever since. One was His Tablets of the Divine Plan, through which the Word of God has come to be promulgated in every land; the other was His Will and Testament, which set in motion a process for the establishment of the Administrative Order. Now, at the close of the first century of the Formative Age, and at the outset of a new series of global Plans, the accelerating progress of the Master's Divine Plan is plain to see. And the organic unfoldment of the Administrative Order over the last hundred years is demonstrated by the existence of the vast array of institutions and agencies, from the international level to the local, that channel the spirit of the Faith and guide and support the efforts of the worldwide Bahá'í community. The Covenant of which 'Abdu'l-Bahá was the Centre remains an impregnable stronghold. We rejoice at how the Covenant orients each believer towards a common mission, maintaining a dynamic unity that cultivates a constantly growing community of the faithful.

Contemplating the Person of the Master, we find 4.7 ourselves wonderstruck by the all-compassing authority that accompanied His inexhaustible patience and understanding, by the keenness of His wisdom in every setting, by the infinite tenderness of His being, and by His limitless love that can be felt by every unshuttered soul. But every prompting to pay homage to His matchless qualities is restrained by the recollection that never did He seek praise or worldly recognition. And so we feel compelled to testify: Beloved of all our hearts, 'Abdu'l-Bahá, Your all was servitude—a servitude "complete, pure and real, firmly established, enduring, obvious, explicitly revealed and subject to no interpretation whatever". We reserve what words remain for a pledge of fidelity to You, for our vow to uphold the Covenant that You "proclaimed, championed and vindicated", for our wholehearted expression of loyalty to Your timeless guidance and expositions, to Your fervent entreaties and exhortations. This same pledge is manifested in the steadfast, strenuous exertions of the Bahá'í world to fulfil the mission entrusted to it at this time. Seeing this community striving to live by Your example summons up for us these words of Yours:

4.8   O friends! Praise be to God that the banner of Divine Unity hath been hoisted in every land, and the melody of the Abhá Kingdom hath been raised on every side. The holy Seraph of the Concourse on high is raising the cry of "Yá Bahá'u'l-Abhá!" in the midmost heart of the world, and the power of the Word of God is breathing true life into the body of existence.

4.9   Wherefore, O ye faithful friends, it behoveth you all to join 'Abdu'l-Bahá in self-sacrifice and in service to the Cause of God and thraldom to His divine Threshold. If ye be aided to attain unto such a supreme bounty, the whole world shall erelong be made the recipient of the effulgent splendours of God, and the longed-for oneness of humanity shall be revealed in the utmost beauty and charm in the midmost heart of the world. This is the dearest wish of 'Abdu'l-Bahá! This is the greatest yearning of them that are faithful! The Glory of Glories rest upon you.

THE UNIVERSAL HOUSE OF JUSTICE

To the Bahá'ís of the World

Dearly loved Friends,

As we reflect on the events which a few days ago   5.1
marked the centenary of the Ascension of 'Abdu'l-Bahá
in the Holy Land, we feel impelled to express to you
our sense of wonderment at the exalted character of
what transpired. We offer praise and gratitude to the
Blessed Beauty that, despite current circumstances in
the world and the many restrictions on travel, nearly
six hundred representatives of the vast majority of
National Spiritual Assemblies and Regional Bahá'í
Councils were able to be present at the Bahá'í World
Centre for this historic occasion. The days of this
remarkable gathering were spent in profound
contemplation on the life and example of the
beloved Master, on 'Abdu'l-Bahá as the Centre of
the Covenant, on His Will and Testament and the
unfoldment of the Administrative Order over the last
century, and on the extraordinary distance the Bahá'í
world has travelled through the implementation of His
Divine Plan. A spirit of consecration permeated the air
as those present prayed in the vicinity of His resting
place on the anniversary of the holy night of His
Ascension. The love of 'Abdu'l-Bahá drew the souls to
the Mountain of the Lord, and they return to their
homes carrying the love of the Universal House of

Justice to the institutions they represent and to all the friends of God.

5.2   We are confident that the spiritual forces generated by this gathering will be diffused throughout your communities and will inspire the friends as they prepare themselves for the upcoming series of worldwide conferences, which will launch the Bahá'í world into the next stage of the Divine Plan. To this end, we will offer our ardent prayers at the Sacred Threshold.

THE UNIVERSAL HOUSE OF JUSTICE

30 December 2021

To the Conference of the
Continental Boards of Counsellors

Dearly loved Friends,

At Riḍván this year we described how, over the 6.1
course of a quarter century, the Bahá'í world underwent a transformation that endowed it with an
undreamed-of capacity to learn, to grow, and to serve
humanity. But, however bright were the achievements
of this period, they must be eclipsed by what is to
come. By the conclusion of the new series of Plans
recently begun, the Bahá'í community will need to
have acquired capacities that can scarcely be glimpsed
at present. In your deliberations over the coming days,
you will be occupied with exploring what is required
to bring into being such a fortified community.

Bahá'u'lláh states that "the purpose for which 6.2
mortal men have, from utter nothingness, stepped into
the realm of being, is that they may work for the
betterment of the world and live together in concord
and harmony." He has revealed teachings that make
this possible. Building a society that consciously pur-
sues this collective purpose is the work of not only
this generation, but of many generations to come, and
Bahá'u'lláh's followers welcome all who labour alongside them in this undertaking. It means learning how

to raise up vibrant, outward-looking communities; it means those communities learning how to bring about spiritual and material progress; it means learning how to contribute to the discourses that influence the direction of that progress. These areas of endeavour are, naturally, familiar ones. Seen from one perspective, they are quite distinct, each having its own characteristics and imperatives. Yet they all represent ways of awakening the energies latent in the human soul and channelling them towards the betterment of society. Together, they are means of releasing what the Guardian described as "the society-building power" of the Faith. This inherent power possessed by the Cause of Bahá'u'lláh is visible even in the fledgling efforts of a Bahá'í community learning to serve humanity and promote the Word of God. And though the world society foreshadowed in His Revelation is of course far distant, communities that are earnestly learning to apply His teachings to their social reality abound. How immensely blessed are those souls who, alive to the greatness of this Day and the significance of their actions, strive for the emergence of a society shaped by the divine teachings.

6.3   The series of global Plans that began at Riḍván will last a full twenty-five years. It will carry the ark of the Cause into the third century of the Bahá'í Era and conclude at Riḍván 2046. During this period, the Bahá'í world will be focused on a single aim: the release of the society-building power of the Faith in ever-greater measures. The pursuit of this overall aim will require a further rise in the capacity of the individual believer, the local community, and the institutions of the Faith. These three constant protagonists of the Plan each have a part to play, and each one has capacities and qualities that must be developed. However, each is incapable of manifesting its full potential on its own. It is by strengthening their dynamic relationships with one another that their powers are combined and multiplied. 'Abdu'l-Bahá explains that the more the qualities of cooperation and mutual assistance are manifested by a people, "the more will human society advance in progress and prosperity"; in the Faith, this principle distinguishes and shapes the interactions of individuals, institutions, and communities, and it endows the body of the Cause with moral vigour and spiritual health.

The enkindled souls being raised up through the processes of the Plan are seeking to gain an ever more profound understanding of Bahá'u'lláh's teachings—"the sovereign remedy for every disease"—and to apply them to the needs of their society. They are committed to the prosperity of all, recognizing that the welfare of individuals rests in the welfare of society at large. They are loyal citizens who eschew partisanship and the contest for worldly power. Instead, they are focused on transcending differences, harmonizing perspectives, and promoting the use of consultation for making decisions. They emphasize qualities and attitudes—such as trustworthiness, cooperation, and forbearance—that are building blocks of a stable social order. They champion rationality and science as essential for human progress. They advocate tolerance and

6.4

understanding, and with the inherent oneness of humanity uppermost in their minds, they view everyone as a potential partner to collaborate with, and they strive to foster fellow feeling even among groups who may traditionally have been hostile to one another. They are conscious of how the forces of materialism are at work around them, and their eyes are wide open to the many injustices that persist in the world, yet they are equally clear sighted about the creative power of unity and humanity's capacity for altruism. They see the power that true religion possesses to transform hearts and overcome distrust, and so, with confidence in what the future holds, they labour to cultivate the conditions in which progress can occur. They share their beliefs liberally with others, remaining respectful of the freedom of conscience of every soul, and they never impose their own standards on anyone. And while they would not pretend to have discovered all the answers, they are clear about what they have learned and what they still need to learn. Their efforts advance to the alternating rhythm of action and reflection; setbacks leave them unfazed. In places where growing numbers are helping to build communities of this character, the power of the Cause to transform people's social existence, as well as their inner lives, is becoming increasingly visible. Earnest pursuit of the Plan's central aim will, we are sure, cause many, many such communities to emerge.

The movement of clusters

A greater expression of the society-building power   6.5
of the Faith requires, first and foremost, still further
advances in the process of entry by troops in every part
of the world. The essentially spiritual undertakings of
diffusing the light of Bahá'u'lláh's Revelation ever
more widely and extending the roots of His Faith ever
more deeply into the soil of society have measurable
outcomes: the number of clusters where a programme
of growth has been initiated and the degree of intensity
that each has reached. The means now exist for a swift
advance in relation to both measures. The goal that the
community of the Greatest Name must aspire to fulfil
during the current series of global Plans is to establish
intensive programmes of growth in all the clusters
in the world. This formidable objective implies a
broadening and intensification of activity on a scale
never witnessed. Rapid progress towards this goal must
be achieved in the course of the Nine Year Plan.

As a preliminary step, we ask that you assist   6.6
National Spiritual Assemblies and Regional Bahá'í
Councils to determine whether their schemes for
dividing their territories into clusters would benefit
from any adjustments. As you know, a cluster defines
an area where the activities of the Plan can be
stimulated in a manageable and sustainable way.
Over the last twenty-one years, much has been learned
about the size of cluster that is "manageable" in
different contexts and in different parts of the world; in
some countries, modifications have already begun to

be considered, occasioned by the effects of growth. In many instances this reassessment will not lead to any change, but in some it will result in a cluster being divided or reduced in size, and occasionally a cluster might become larger. Areas that are sparsely populated owing to the natural terrain may be excluded from the clustering scheme. Of course, any believers who reside in such places would adopt as many elements of the framework for action as are applicable to their circumstances.

6.7   The movement of clusters along a continuum of development will remain the basic model for the expansion and consolidation of the community. The features of the developmental path that should be followed, and in particular the first, second, and third milestones that mark progress along the way, are already well known to the friends from our previous messages and from their own experience, and we feel no need to reiterate what we have stated before. By the close of the One Year Plan we anticipate that programmes of growth will be under way in over 6,000 clusters, that in close to 5,000 of these the second milestone will have been passed, and that in 1,300 of these the believers will have advanced further. These figures must climb considerably over the coming nine years. Once any adjustments to the clustering scheme in each country have been determined, we ask that you work with National Assemblies and Regional Councils to forecast the numbers of clusters where progress could be made past the first, second, and third milestones, respectively, during the Plan. It should be borne in mind that these are only intended to be well-informed estimates; they can be refined later as necessary and need not be laboured over at length. As such, we request that the results of these assessments be sent to the Bahá'í World Centre by Naw-Rúz. At Riḍván, we will then be able to set out the total collective aspirations of the Bahá'í world for the Nine Year Plan.

We are conscious that there are some regions and 6.8 countries where the Faith remains at an early point of development, and there is a pressing need to ensure that what the Bahá'í world has learned about accelerating the growth process benefits these places as well. One important lesson that has become clear is the immense value, to a region, of a cluster where the third milestone has been passed. Once the friends in a given cluster have developed the range of capacities that such progress implies, and the means to disseminate insights and share experience about community-building endeavours are in place, then a swift acceleration of the work of expansion and consolidation in surrounding clusters becomes possible. With this in mind, it is imperative that during the Nine Year Plan the process of growth reach this level of intensity in at least one cluster in every country and every region. This constitutes one of the Plan's chief objectives and it will call for the concentrated effort of many a consecrated soul. The International Teaching Centre is ready to work with you to implement several strategies to bring this about. Foremost among these will be the deployment of teams of international and homefront pioneers who are familiar with the framework for action and are prepared to dedicate significant amounts of time and energy to serving the Cause over a number of years. You will need to impress upon National Spiritual Assemblies and Regional Bahá'í Councils the urgency of encouraging believers who, following in the footsteps of so many heroic souls of the past, can arise to ensure that the light of the Faith shines bright in every territory. We look in particular to countries, regions, and clusters where strength and experience have accumulated to generate a flow of pioneers to places where help is needed, and also to provide support by other means. This flow of support is one more way in which the spirit of collaboration and mutual assistance, so essential for progress, manifests itself in systematic action.

6.9   The accomplishments of the previous series of Plans—particularly the last Five Year Plan—could not have occurred without a tremendous advance in the teaching work. An important dimension of this work is the capacity to engage in conversations on spiritual themes, a capacity which was explored in our message to your 2015 conference, where we described how it is developed through participation in institute courses and by gaining practical experience. It is evident that the pattern of activity unfolding at the grassroots opens up a variety of settings in which receptive souls—sometimes whole families or peer groups—can take part in meaningful conversations which awaken interest in the vision of the Faith and the Person of Bahá'u'lláh. Over time, many such souls begin to identify themselves with the Bahá'í community, especially as they gain the confidence to participate in community life through service. Of course, the community welcomes any degree of association that a person would like to maintain, great or small. Yet to recognize Bahá'u'lláh as a Manifestation of God and accept the privileges and responsibilities that are uniquely associated with membership in the Bahá'í community is a singular moment in a person's spiritual development, quite distinct from regular involvement in Bahá'í activities or voicing support for Bahá'í principles. Experience has shown that the environment created by community-building endeavours in a locality enables anyone who wishes to take this step to do so with relative ease. Wherever these endeavours are under way, it is important for the friends to remain mindful that the doors of the Faith are wide open and to give encouragement to those who stand at the threshold. And in areas where such endeavours have been well established for some time, many believers are discovering that a vibrant, expanding pattern of activity can naturally lead to families, groups of friends, and even clusters of households being ready to enter the Cause. For in spaces where the possibility of joining the community can be discussed openly and inclusively among those who share a sense of collective identity, souls can more easily feel emboldened to take this step together. Bahá'í institutions, especially Local Spiritual Assemblies, must adopt a mindset that allows for such developments, and ensure that any obstacles are removed.

6.10   We ask you and your auxiliaries to help the believers, wherever they reside, reflect periodically on effective ways of teaching the Faith in their surroundings, and to fan within their hearts a passion for teaching that will attract the confirmations of the Divine Kingdom. Souls who have been given the blessing of faith have a natural wish to share this gift through conversations with relatives, friends, classmates, co-workers, and those previously unmet, seeking in every place and at every moment a hearing ear. Different settings and circumstances lend themselves to different approaches, and the friends should be occupied in an ongoing process of learning about what is most effective in the place where they are.

Learning from the most advanced clusters

6.11   Six years ago we described for you the characteristics of a cluster where the friends have passed the third milestone along the continuum of growth. To have come this far implies intense activity occurring in specific neighbourhoods or villages, but also concerted effort being made by the generality of the believers living across the cluster—in other words, a rising spirit of universal participation in the work of community building. In practice, this means the mobilization of a sizeable number of Bahá'ís who are creatively and intelligently applying the Plan's framework for action to the reality of their own circumstances wherever in the cluster they live. It entails families and individual believers working together and making a conscious decision to see themselves as belonging to an expand-

48

ing nucleus. Such groups of friends set about widening the circle of participation in their activities by engaging with the networks to which they belong—networks created through a place of work or study, a local school, or a community hub of another kind—and by accompanying others who arise to serve alongside them. These efforts have tremendous merit. Even when a cluster contains a number of flourishing centres of intense activity, efforts being made across the rest of the cluster might still represent a large proportion of all the activity that is occurring. We also acknowledge, in this connection, the steps being taken in some clusters to systematically reach out to a specific population that has shown receptivity to the Faith but is dispersed throughout the cluster. This can be seen as a specialized form of the community-building work, and one which continues to show great promise. As participation in the work of the Plan in all its forms increases, many opportunities emerge for the friends to learn from each other's experience and to kindle within one another the joy of teaching.

Of course, the work undertaken in receptive neigh- 6.12
bourhoods and villages has been a special focus of attention in recent years. As the inhabitants of such locations begin to participate in Bahá'í activities in large numbers, more consideration needs to be given to coordination in order to cope with the inherent complexity involved. Within each centre of intense activity, collaborative arrangements emerge among groups of families, who organize community-building activities among themselves with a view to widening

the embrace of such activities to many nearby households; an informal network of friends provides encouragement and support to the endeavours under way. The character of daily life in such places is adapting to the rise of a culture in which worship and service are cherished activities involving many people at once. Uplifting, well-prepared community gatherings—extending in some cases to camps and festivals—occur with increasing frequency, and music and song feature prominently on such occasions. Indeed the arts as a whole, so integral a part of the development of a community from the start, stand out in such settings as an important means of generating joy, strengthening bonds of unity, disseminating knowledge, and consolidating understanding, as well as of acquainting those in the wider society with the principles of the Cause. And naturally, there remains a strong focus on being outward looking: finding ways to continually share the fruits of a thriving pattern of action with souls who are as yet unfamiliar with the Faith.

6.13   Amid all this, we have observed a specific, heartening phenomenon, whose early glimpses we described in our message to your 2015 conference as representing a new frontier. Although learning how to embrace large numbers is a characteristic of any cluster where the third milestone has been passed, the focus of the friends necessarily begins to broaden as they approach a point where a significant proportion of the population of a particular area is taking part in community-building activities. This might be true for only a specific residential area in a cluster, or for several such areas, or for a single village; other parts of the cluster might not yet share the same reality. But in such locations, the thoughts of the friends labouring at the grassroots are increasingly occupied with the progress and well-being of everyone dwelling in the vicinity. Bahá'í institutions feel more keenly their responsibility for the spiritual education of an entire generation of children and junior youth, most or even all of whom might already be engaged in community activities. Local Spiritual Assemblies strengthen their relationships with authorities and local leaders, even entering into formal collaborations, and growing attention is given to the multiplying initiatives of social action arising from groups of junior youth, youth, women, families, or others who are responding to the needs around them. The sheer level and variety of activity requires Auxiliary Board members to appoint multiple assistants to serve a single village or neighbourhood; each assistant might follow one or more lines of action, offering counsel and support as necessary, and lending momentum to the processes in motion.

In places where the activities of the Plan have 6.14 reached such a degree of prevalence, the inhabitants now possess a substantially increased capacity to steer the course of their own development, and the institutions and agencies of the Faith there now have an expanded vision of their responsibilities. Of course, these responsibilities still include having robust systems in place to continually build capacity and support those taking initiative. But the advancement of the community depends, to a greater extent than before, on local institutions and agencies being conscious of the social forces at work in the environment and acting to preserve the integrity of the community's many endeavours. Meanwhile, the relationship of the Bahá'í community to the surrounding society undergoes profound change. As represented by its formal structures of administration and informal collaborative arrangements, the Bahá'í community has become a highly visible protagonist in society in its own right, one that is ready to shoulder important responsibilities and intensify a broad, collective process of learning about spiritual and material progress. At the same time, as the wider society embraces many aspects of Bahá'í community life and imbibes its unifying spirit, the dynamics thus created allow divers groups to come together in a combined movement inspired by Bahá'u'lláh's vision of the oneness of humanity. To date, the number of places where a Bahá'í pattern of community life has attained such prevalence is modest, yet it is growing. Here is witnessed a release of the society-building power of the Faith unlike anything that has been seen before.

6.15   Naturally, prevalence of Bahá'í activity on this scale is not a prospect everywhere. It is necessary to appreciate the difference that is made by the conditions in a cluster or in parts of a cluster and by the characteristics of a people—that is, by the reality of circumstances. Accordingly, the ways in which the society-building power of the Faith will find expression in different settings will vary. But regardless of the extent to which

Bahá'í community life embraces those who reside in a particular area—regardless, even, of the intensity of a programme of growth in a cluster or the level of activity in a neighbourhood or village—the challenge facing the friends serving at the grassroots is essentially the same in every place. They must be able to read their own reality and ask: what, in light of the possibilities and requirements at hand, would be fitting objectives to pursue in the coming cycle or series of cycles? You and your auxiliaries are ideally placed to put this question and to ensure that appropriate strategies are identified. Much can be learned from the experience of the friends in similar clusters, for a community that is a step further along the same path can provide valuable insights about the goal to strive for next. As the friends ponder what is before them, they will readily see that for every community there is a goal in reach, and for every goal a path to reach it. Looking ahead on this path, might we not perceive Bahá'u'lláh Himself, the reins of humanity's affairs in one hand, His other beckoning all to hasten, hasten?

Contributing to social transformation

The Revelation of Bahá'u'lláh is concerned with the   6.16
transformation of both humanity's inner life and
social environment. A letter written on behalf of
Shoghi Effendi describes how the social environment
provides the "atmosphere" in which souls can "grow
spiritually and reflect in full the light of God" shining
through the Revelation. A clear sign that the society-
building power of the Cause is being released in a

cluster is that efforts are being made by a growing band of its inhabitants, inspired by the teachings of the Faith, to help improve the spiritual character and social conditions of the wider community to which they belong. The contribution made by Bahá'ís is distinguished by its focus on building capacity for service; it is an approach founded on faith in the ability of a population to become the protagonists of their own development.

6.17 As the intensity of community-building work in a cluster increases, the friends there inevitably become more conscious of social, economic, or cultural barriers that are impeding people's spiritual and material progress. Children and junior youth lacking support in their education, pressures on girls resulting from traditional customs related to early marriage, families needing help with navigating unfamiliar systems of healthcare, a village struggling for want of some basic necessity, or long-standing prejudices arising from a legacy of hostility between different groups—when a Bahá'í community's efforts in the field of expansion and consolidation bring it into contact with these situations and many others, it will be drawn to respond to such realities as its circumstances permit. In reflecting on such situations it becomes evident that, within clusters, expansion and consolidation, social action, and contributing to prevalent discourses are dimensions of a single, unified, outward-looking endeavour carried out at the grassroots of society. All these efforts are pursued according to a common framework for action, and this above all else brings coherence to the overall pattern of activity.

The initial stirrings of grassroots social action 6.18 begin to be seen in a cluster as the availability of human resources increases and capacity for a wider range of tasks develops. Villages have proven to be notably fertile ground from which social action initiatives have emerged and been sustained, but in urban settings too, friends living there have succeeded in carrying out activities and projects suited to the social environment, at times by working with local schools, agencies of civil society, or even government bodies. Social action is being undertaken in a number of important fields, including the environment, agriculture, health, the arts, and particularly education. Over the course of the Nine Year Plan, and especially as the study of specific institute courses stimulates greater activity in this area, we expect to see a proliferation of formal and informal efforts to promote the social and economic development of a people. Some of these community-based initiatives will require basic administrative structures to sustain their work. Where conditions are propitious, Local Spiritual Assemblies will need to be encouraged to learn how best to cultivate new, fledgling initiatives and to foster efforts that show promise. In some cases, the needs associated with a particular field of endeavour will warrant the establishment of a Bahá'í-inspired organization, and we anticipate the appearance of more such organizations during the coming Plan. For their part, National Spiritual Assemblies will have to find ways in which they can stay well informed about what is being learned at the grassroots of their communities and analyse the experience being gained; in some places this will call for the creation of an entity dedicated to following social action. Looking across the Bahá'í world, we are delighted to see how much momentum has already been generated in this area of endeavour through the encouragement and support of the Bahá'í International Development Organization.

6.19   Closely connected with the capacity for engaging in social action is a capacity for contributing to the discourses of society. At heart, this is simply a capacity for participating in a conversation about a matter that affects people's lives and offering a perspective grounded in Bahá'í principles and Bahá'í experience. Viewed in this way, it is a skill which many Bahá'ís have the opportunity to practise almost daily, for instance in their studies or occupations, and which is cultivated through involvement in institute courses; in its more formal expression, it is central to the work of the Bahá'í International Community and national Offices of External Affairs. However, in relation to the release of the society-building power of the Faith at the grassroots, it is a capacity that comes into greater demand as closer association with a population, brought about through the work of expansion and consolidation, leads to increased consciousness of an area's prevailing social problems, as well as of the aspirations of its people to overcome them. As the number of those participating in community-building activities rises, so does the need for the Bahá'í community to offer, as a unified body, its considered perspective on obstacles to social progress and on issues that weigh on the minds and spirits of those with whom it interacts. This has particular implications for Local Spiritual Assemblies. In places where the activities of the Plan have attained a degree of prevalence, the Assembly begins to be viewed more widely as a source of moral insight. Over time, efforts to contribute to societal discourses become more systematic, and Bahá'ís become adept at helping those around them to engage constructively in a discourse and find consensus. Opportunities are sought out to share the perspectives of the Faith with community leaders and figures in authority, and spaces are created in which representatives of various groups and interests can be assisted to reach a common point of view through consultation. We are pleased with the steps that have already been taken to learn how insights from the Revelation of Bahá'u'lláh and from the experience of Bahá'í communities can be brought to bear upon pressing social issues at the local level; much more is sure to be learned in this regard during the Nine Year Plan.

We wish to stress that, historically and now, 6.20 social action and efforts to participate in the prevalent discourses of society have emerged not only in the context of growth, but also as a result of individual Bahá'ís striving to contribute to society's progress in ways available to them. As a personal response to Bahá'u'lláh's summons to work for the betterment of the world, believers have variously chosen to adopt certain vocations and have sought out opportunities to support the activities of like-minded groups and organizations. Projects, both large and small, have been started in order to respond to a range of social issues. Numerous Bahá'í-inspired organizations have been established by groups of individuals to work for many different objectives, and specialist entities have been founded to give attention to a particular discourse. All of these efforts, at whatever scale they have been undertaken, have benefited from being able to draw on the principles and insights guiding the activities occurring at the grassroots of the worldwide Bahá'í community, and they have also benefited from the wise counsels of Local and National Spiritual Assemblies. We rejoice to see these diverse, harmonious expressions of faith by the devoted followers of the Blessed Beauty, in response to the tribulations of a perplexed and sorely agitated world.

Educational endeavours and the training institute

6.21   The importance of education to a Bahá'í conception of spiritual and social transformation can hardly be overestimated. "Consider", Bahá'u'lláh states, "the revelation of the light of the Name of God, the Educator. Behold, how in all things the evidences of such a revelation are manifest, how the betterment of all beings dependeth upon it." The significance of education in the work of community building is unmistakable, and in the field of social action the provision of education remains the signature contribution of Bahá'ís in most parts of the world. Pre-eminent among the structures and agencies created by the Bahá'í world to offer education is, of course, the training institute. Indeed, the network of national and regional training institutes operating with such proficiency around the globe is among the choicest fruits of the previous series of global Plans. Building capacity for service within communities by enabling ever-increasing numbers of individuals to benefit from the institute process will continue to be a central feature of the Plans in the present series. The capacity for community development that has already emerged, represented by hundreds of thousands of individuals who are able to serve as tutors, animators, or children's class teachers, is a resource of historic consequence.

When we first introduced the concept of the training institute, it was in the context of the need to raise up human resources to take on the tasks of expansion and consolidation. At this juncture, when a new series of Plans has just begun, we invite you to take a more expansive view. Increasingly, participation in institute courses is preparing the friends of God for an ever-deeper engagement in the life of the wider community; it is endowing them with the knowledge, insights, and skills that enable them to contribute not only to the process of developing their own community, but to the progress of society. In short, the institute is a potent means for the society-building power of the Faith to find release. Although the task of developing curricular materials to support this purpose is a long-term undertaking, existing materials already aim to build capacity for a broad range of initiatives. Moreover, they offer a seamless coherent 6.22

educational experience from the age of five, upwards to the age of junior youth, and through into adulthood, and they serve as a direct counterpart to the pattern of activities unfolding at the grassroots. In relation to this, we have been pleased to see the rich insights that the friends in different parts of the world, in a variety of social and cultural contexts, are generating about aspects of community development. If these insights, and those still to emerge, are to benefit Bahá'í communities more widely, systems for the preparation and refinement of educational materials will need to be extended. With this in mind, we will soon set out the approach that will guide this work over the coming years.

6.23   With respect to raising the capacity of institutes to deliver each of the three stages of the educational process, we are glad to see that attention is increasingly being given to enhancing the quality of the educational experience itself, in addition to expanding the system for its delivery. A critical requirement is to enable all those contributing to the work of the institute to progressively advance their understanding of the educational content: its objectives, its structure, its pedagogical principles, its methodology, its central concepts, its interconnections. Many training institute boards have been supported in this regard by the collaborative groups described in our message to your 2015 conference. In places, separate teams have also begun to focus respectively on children's classes, junior youth groups, and study circles, identifying factors that contribute to their effectiveness and finding ways to assist the friends involved in each avenue of service to further raise their own capacity. The Auxiliary Board members in a region and their assistants are often the first to see to it that what is being learned reaches a wider number of friends across adjoining clusters and within centres of intense activity. Individuals with a depth of experience in the promotion of institute activities are serving as resource persons, and they have proved instrumental in helping institutes at an earlier point of development to advance. Nevertheless, in general it is Counsellors who are ensuring that each institute becomes familiar with the many essential insights being generated by their sister agencies in neighbouring countries and regions. Counsellors have arranged for institutes to be organized into groupings of varying sizes to enable the lessons that are being learned by the most experienced institutes to be shared more widely, increasingly through the means of formal seminars. All these arrangements will need to be strengthened during the next Plan. In places where a site for the dissemination of learning about the junior youth spiritual empowerment programme is operating, collaboration between the learning site and associated institutes has already proved extremely fruitful, and it should intensify; their pursuit of a common goal and their shared desire to see clusters advance create ideal conditions for the spirit of cooperation and mutual assistance to flourish. The knowledge that has now accumulated about factors that contribute to the effectiveness of the institute process is extensive, and we look to the International Teaching Centre to

organize what has been learned and make it available
to you.

6.24   What we have described above is an educational
system in a state of constant refinement. This requires
many individuals to lend their support to its further
development; it also requires institutes, and Bahá'í
institutions more generally, to plan ahead and ensure
that individuals who have developed considerable
capacity in supporting the community's educational
endeavours are able to sustain their service and can,
when their life circumstances change, continue to
be involved in the work of the institute in other
meaningful ways. Appreciating the effectiveness of
the institute process, every follower of Bahá'u'lláh will
feel a desire to contribute to its advancement in some
way—not least, the Bahá'í youth. Institutes know well
that releasing the potential possessed by young people
is, for them, a sacred charge; we now ask that Bahá'í
youth view the future development of the institute in
the very same light. At the vanguard of a nine-year,
community-wide endeavour to bring the institute to
a higher level of functioning, we expect to see a
broad movement of youth setting the standard.
They should seize every opportunity—in their schools
and universities, and in spaces dedicated to work,
family, or social interaction—to encourage more and
more souls to benefit from the institute's programmes.
Some youth will be able to devote a period of service—
perhaps even successive years—to the provision of
education, especially to those younger than themselves;
for many, support for the institute's activities will be

an ever-present dimension of their lives throughout their own education and as they seek a livelihood from their calling in this world; but for none should it be anything less than a cherished commitment.

In many parts of the world, a natural outcome of 6.25 the participation of individuals and families in the institute process has been an increased consciousness of the importance of education in all its forms. Friends serving as children's class teachers take a keen interest in the broad educational development of those they teach, while friends serving as tutors and animators are naturally concerned with the extent to which those approaching or entering adulthood—girls and boys alike—can access and benefit from education of many kinds, not limited to the courses offered by the institute itself. For instance, they can encourage young people to look towards apprenticeships or university studies. We have been struck by how, in many communities, engagement in the institute process by large numbers has gradually reshaped this aspect of culture within a population. The institutions of the Faith will need to take responsibility for ensuring that, as consciousness is raised in this way, the noble aspirations that arise in young people as a result—aspirations to acquire the education and training that will allow them to offer a lifetime of meaningful service to their society—can be fulfilled. The long-term development of a community and, ultimately, of a nation, from generation to generation, depends to a large degree on the effort made to invest in those who will assume responsibility for collective social progress.

6.26   This exploration of the centrality of education to a community founded on Bahá'í principles would be incomplete without a further observation. Shoghi Effendi has laid great stress on the importance of striving, through "constant endeavour", to obtain "a more adequate understanding of the significance of Bahá'u'lláh's stupendous Revelation". The training institute has no parallel as an instrument for the systematic exposure of limitless numbers of souls to the life-giving waters of the Revelation and the inexhaustible meaning of the Word of God. But the friends' efforts to increase their understanding of the Faith and its teachings are of course not limited to participation in the institute process. Indeed, one strong indicator of an institute's effectiveness is the thirst it cultivates within those who engage with its materials to continue to study the Cause of Bahá'u'lláh—individually, but also collectively, whether in formal spaces created by the institutions or in more informal settings. Beyond the study of the Revelation itself, the implications that the teachings hold for countless fields of human endeavour are of great importance. A notable example of one form of education through which young believers are becoming better acquainted with a Bahá'í perspective on issues relevant to the progress of humanity is participation in the seminars offered by the Institute for Studies in Global Prosperity. Given the vastness of the ocean of the Revelation, it will be apparent that exploring its depths is a lifelong occupation of every soul who would tread the path of service.

As the contribution being made by the Faith to the   6.27
progress of society in different parts of the world
gains greater visibility, the Bahá'í community will
increasingly be called upon to explicate the principles
it advocates, and to demonstrate their applicability to
the issues facing humanity. The more the intellectual
life of a community blossoms and thrives, the greater
its capacity to answer this call. It will be up to the
followers of Bahá'u'lláh to provide, in the world of
ideas, the intellectual rigour and clarity of thought to
match their commitment to spiritual and material
progress in the world of deeds.

Raising capacity for administration at all levels

Eighty years ago, a letter written on behalf of the   6.28
Guardian described Bahá'í administration as "the first
shaping of what in future will come to be the social life
and laws of community living". Today, at the beginning
of the second century of the Formative Age, the shape
of Bahá'í administration has developed considerably,
and its continued development will be essential for the
release of the society-building power of the Faith.

The administration of the Faith at the grassroots is,   6.29
of course, intimately connected with the development
of Local Spiritual Assemblies. These nascent Houses
of Justice are described by Shoghi Effendi as "the
chief sinews of Bahá'í society, as well as the ultimate
foundation of its administrative structure", and he
greatly emphasizes the importance of their formation.
In 1995, we called for the reinstitution of the practice

that required all Local Assemblies, including those being newly formed, to be elected on the First Day of Riḍván rather than at any other time of year. This development was related to the fact that, while believers from outside a locality could assist with the electoral process, the primary responsibility for electing any Assembly and maintaining its operations rests with the Bahá'ís of that place; much depends on their readiness for undertaking administrative activity. It has been seen, in recent years, how a sense of Bahá'í identity can gradually gain strength in an area as a pattern of action grounded in the teachings becomes established among individuals and families living there. Thus, a community will often have attained a certain level of capacity in relation to community-building endeavours by the time the formation of a Local Assembly becomes possible. As this point approaches—and it should not be unduly delayed—efforts have to be made to cultivate an appreciation for the formal aspects of community life associated with Bahá'í administration. The Local Assembly that emerges in such a milieu is likely to be well aware of its responsibility to encourage and strengthen those activities which help to sustain a vibrant community. However, it will also need to gain proficiency in discharging a wide range of other responsibilities, and the support provided to it by your auxiliaries and their assistants will be vitally important. In our message to your 2010 conference, we described the developmental path of such an Assembly, and we referred to various dimensions of its functioning that would need to receive attention, including its ability to manage and develop a Local Fund and, in time, to support initiatives of social action and to interact with agencies of local government and civil society. The benefits that accrue to a community being served by such an Assembly need no elaboration.

In your interactions with National Spiritual 6.30 Assemblies and Regional Bahá'í Councils, we ask that you devote attention to the matter of establishing Local Spiritual Assemblies and consolidating their operations, especially in areas where this aspect of growth may have received less emphasis. We anticipate this will contribute to a rapid rise in the number of Local Assemblies formed year on year. In some countries, your consultations will need to include consideration of whether in rural areas existing arrangements for defining the boundaries of each locality are adequate.

One compelling insight which has emerged is that 6.31 the extent to which the station and leadership of a Local Assembly is recognized in a community is related to how deeply the believers appreciate the sacredness of the electoral process and their duty to participate in it, in an atmosphere wholly free from the taint of suasion or worldly attitudes about power. As consciousness is raised in a community about the spiritual principles underlying Bahá'í elections, a new conception is formed of what it means for someone to be called to serve on an institution, and understanding grows of how the individual, the community, and the Local Assembly and its agencies relate to one another. Where systematic effort has been made to stimulate conversations in a community about the formation of the Local Assembly and its purpose, and to sustain those conversations year after year, the strength of the elected body and the dynamism of community life reinforce each other.

6.32 This reciprocal effect has been especially noticeable over the last two years in places where we have approved the adoption of a two-stage electoral process for a Local Spiritual Assembly, an approach which traces its origins to instructions given by 'Abdu'l-Bahá to the Spiritual Assembly of Ṭihrán. Twenty-two Local Assemblies, spread over eight countries, have already begun to be elected by this method during this period. Similar in many respects to the election of a National Spiritual Assembly, it involves the division of a locality into units from each of which one or more delegates are elected, after which the delegates elect the members of the Local Assembly. As the number of Bahá'ís residing in a locality grows large and the community's capacity for managing complexity increases, the case for implementing a two-stage electoral process becomes commensurately stronger. Accordingly, in the coming Plan, we expect to authorize the adoption of this method for electing a Local Assembly in many more places, both urban and rural, where conditions make such a step timely.

6.33 A Local Spiritual Assembly maintains a keen interest in learning how best to advance the community-building work within its jurisdiction, and as such it consults regularly with friends involved in coordinating endeavours in the cluster. It follows closely the development of any centres of intense activity in the locality, especially by offering support to the teams of believers who have emerged there and are stimulating the process of growth. In general, the more the intensification of activity requires organizational arrangements at the level of the locality or in parts of the locality—say, arranging campaigns of home visits, accompanying families who are holding devotional meetings, or encouraging them to form groups to work together—the more prominent the role that can be assumed by the Local Assembly in this regard. In localities where large numbers are being welcomed into the embrace of Bahá'í activities, and where the complexity of an Assembly's work and manifold responsibilities is increasing, the Assembly sometimes finds that its Secretary needs to be supported by a staffed office, and eventually, the need for a befitting local Ḥaẓíratu'l-Quds becomes more pressing.

As Local Assemblies begin to take on a greater 6.34 and greater share of responsibility for nurturing the development of the community, institutions at the regional and national levels must become more systematic in their efforts to support them. We have been pleased to see this need being addressed in methodical ways, for instance by National Assemblies or Regional Councils convening periodic meetings with the Secretaries and other officers of Local Assemblies to consult about the unfoldment of specific lines of action.

6.35   Where a Regional Council has developed an enhanced capacity for administration, including an ability to provide appropriate kinds of support to many clusters at once, this has been conducive to the accelerated progress of the whole region. Our message to your 2015 conference indicated that in smaller countries where the establishment of Regional Councils is not required, a formal structure would need to emerge at the national level which would be charged with helping clusters to advance. We ask that, in countries where this has not yet occurred, you now consult with National Assemblies about the steps that can be taken to appoint that formal structure, namely, a National Growth Committee with three, five, or seven members. The National Assembly will need to give this agency the necessary latitude to foster the movement of clusters, drawing relevant insights from what has been learned about Regional Councils in this regard. Its responsibilities can include appointing Area Teaching Committees and encouraging them in their plans, arranging for the deployment of homefront pioneers, supporting teaching projects, and distributing core literature. The Committee will benefit from being able to collaborate closely with the training institute, itself an agency of the National Assembly, and with the Auxiliary Board members serving the country, and it will also be able to communicate directly with the relevant Counsellor. While a National Assembly will naturally wish to maintain an ongoing familiarity with the work of the Committee and provide it with guidance, support, and encouragement, creating an entity that is wholly occupied with promoting growth should enable an Assembly to give greater attention to other important matters. In countries where Councils have not been formed but could be established eventually, a National Growth Committee should also be appointed at this time.

As the spiritual energies released by earnest pursuit 6.36 of the Plan surge, they meet resistance from the countervailing forces that hold humanity back from attaining full maturity. In the face of such forces, the vitality of the various lines of action being followed at the local level needs to be preserved and fortified. This critical responsibility is of special relevance to the members of the two Auxiliary Boards, whose numerous, demanding duties keep them closely connected to conditions at the grassroots and alert to anything that might affect the spirit of a community. Across different cultures and social environments, they must assist the friends to face different kinds of challenges: to help previously antagonistic groups find unity through pursuit of a common goal; to learn to put aside inherited customs and attitudes that belong to humanity's period of adolescence, and to overcome prejudices of all kinds; to guard against any tendency to view matters with cynicism or an eye for faults, and instead sustain an eager and constructive outlook; to put the equality of women and men into practice; to cast off inertia and apathy through the exercise of individual initiative; to put one's support of plans for collective action before feelings of personal preference; to harness the power of modern technologies without succumbing to their potentially enervating effects; to prize the sweetness of teaching the Faith and the joy of serving humankind above worldly interests; to reject the opiate of consumerism; to turn away from materialist ideologies and the worldviews they aggressively promote, and fix one's gaze upon the bright beacon that is the laws and principles of God. These, and many more besides, constitute a formidable set of responsibilities for the company of the faithful to fulfil as they navigate what are sure to be tumultuous years in the life of humanity. Your auxiliaries, who have so creditably acquitted themselves in advancing the process of entry by troops, must be equal to all such challenges whenever and wherever they arise. Through the power of their good example and the clarity of their good counsel, may they help the friends to grow in faith, assurance, and commitment to a life of service, and accompany them as they build communities that are havens of peace, places where a harried and conflict-scarred humanity may find shelter.

6.37   Over the last series of Plans, the community's capacity to maintain focus on the Faith's most pressing needs emerged as one of its most important strengths. However, this sense of focus has to accommodate many lines of action, all of which must advance without being in competition. This calls for an expanded vision, a nuanced understanding of coexisting imperatives, added flexibility, and heightened institutional collaboration. We are conscious that the Faith's resources are finite, and individuals experience many demands on their time. But as the Plan unfolds in a given place and the ranks of those who are willing to serve swell, the varied aspects of a rich and vibrant Bahá'í community life will advance in step, and the society-building power of the Faith shine forth.

A historic mission

We hope to have impressed upon you, in these 6.38 pages, that the present-day capacity of the Bahá'í community, combined with the discipline it has achieved through adherence to a coherent framework for action, has prepared it for an extensive, rigorous test of all its resources, spiritual as well as material. The Plan that will shortly commence—the first major undertaking in a sacred twenty-five-year venture, generational in its scope and significance—will make demands of the individual believer, the community, and the institutions reminiscent of the demands that the Guardian made of the Bahá'í world at the outset of the Ten Year Crusade. If, by the grace of Almighty God, the friends should succeed in reaching the heights of heroism to which they are now summoned, history will assuredly pay tribute to their actions in terms no less glowing than those with which it honours the glorious deeds that decorate the annals of the first century of the Formative Age.

We put great reliance on you and on National 6.39 Spiritual Assemblies to ensure that, in all the efforts made to acquaint the friends with the nature of this collective enterprise, the perspective of history is kept fully in view. The civilization of today, for all its material prowess, has been found wanting, and the verdict has been issued by the Supreme Pen: "Know ye not that We have rolled up that which the people possessed, and have unfolded a new order in its place?" The establishment of Divine Civilization is, in the words of the Guardian, "the primary mission of the Bahá'í Faith". It is to be built upon the most foundational qualities, ones for which the world stands in great need: unity, trustworthiness, mutual support, collaboration, fellow feeling, selflessness, commitment to truth, a sense of responsibility, a thirst to learn, the love of an all-embracing heart.

6.40   How we long to see humanity illumined with the love of its Lord; how we long to hear His praise on every tongue. Knowing the ardency of our wish, you know then the emotion with which, when we lay our heads upon the Most Holy Threshold, we implore Bahá'u'lláh to make you, and all who cherish His precious Faith, ever more perfect channels of His ineffable grace.

THE UNIVERSAL HOUSE OF JUSTICE

1 January 2022

To all National Spiritual Assemblies

Dearly loved Friends,

Over the twenty-five-year period that ended at 7.1
Riḍván 2021, the endeavours of training institutes to
help the friends enhance their capacity for service were
central to progress. When, at the beginning of the last
series of global Plans, we called for systematic attention
to be given to devising methods for training large numbers
of believers, institutes faced the task of developing
their own materials or selecting from those readily
available. Generally, institutes found it challenging to
develop new materials; however, those that adopted
the courses prepared by the Ruhi Institute were able to
make rapid progress. Therefore, as was stated in our
message to you of 28 December 2005, we determined
that the books of the Ruhi Institute, which had proven
their efficacy, would constitute the main sequence
of courses of institutes everywhere at least for the
remainder of that series of Plans. The extensive use of
these courses, as well as of the lessons and texts for
the spiritual education of children and junior youth,
expedited the advance of the institute process across
the globe. Now, with the Bahá'í world embarked on a
new series of global Plans, we have considered again
the question of the materials of training institutes and
wish to convey our conclusions.

7.2   The knowledge and insights, the spiritual qualities and attitudes, and the skills and abilities for service treated in the courses of the Ruhi Institute remain vital to the efforts of Bahá'í communities. Therefore, these materials will continue to be a prominent feature of the educational endeavours of all training institutes during this new series of global Plans. We are aware that the Ruhi Institute will, during the Nine Year Plan, seek to complete the preparation of all the materials it has outlined for use in children's classes, junior youth groups, and study circles, and the revision of published editions as necessary in light of experience. However, beyond what it has already delineated, it is not expected to develop new materials to be used worldwide.

7.3   In our message dated 30 December 2021 to the Conference of the Continental Boards of Counsellors, we highlighted how pleased we have been to observe the rich body of knowledge and insights which the friends, labouring in diverse social and cultural contexts, are generating about aspects of the community-building process. The friends are also becoming increasingly adept at identifying needs related to growth that are emerging naturally from efforts at the grassroots. These developments have implications for the systems for preparing and refining educational materials. We have thus concluded that it would now be propitious for more attention to be paid to extending the capacity to prepare educational materials, particularly in relation to supplementary materials and branch courses.

When we addressed the question of materials for 7.4
the education of children and junior youth in our
message to you of 12 December 2011, we indicated
that, beyond the materials that are the core of each of
these programmes, teachers and animators would,
often in consultation with the institute coordinator at
the cluster level, determine whether or not additional
elements would be required to reinforce the educational process. The impressive advances in many parts
of the world with regard to offering spiritual education
to large numbers of children and junior youth have
certainly involved a growing capacity of teachers and
animators to wisely supplement the study of the lessons
and texts with appropriate elements on the basis of
their specific circumstances. Notable in this respect are
elements related to artistic activity and service projects.
Nonetheless, when the need to supplement the study
of a particular topic has been felt across a country or
region, some institutes have themselves developed or
adopted additional materials and have arranged for
them to be disseminated more extensively. These
supplementary items have, for the most part, been simple
elements, such as songs or stories. A similar experience
is unfolding in relation to the main sequence of
courses, although the additional materials that some
institutes have introduced in this connection, which
include compilations from the Bahá'í writings on
specific topics and case studies of relevant experience,
tend to be of a more complex nature.

The flourishing of a vibrant process of spiritual 7.5
education in growing numbers of clusters will require

of institutes a well-developed ability to oversee the appropriate introduction of supplementary elements. In this, institutes must be as much concerned with reinforcing the educational process as with maintaining its integrity. They will thus need to bear in mind the various cautions we set out in our 12 December 2011 message. They must, of course, also guard against overwhelming the friends with diverse additional elements that, by their sheer volume, might inadvertently detract from the effective delivery of the principal materials.

7.6   Concerning branch courses, how they are to emerge must be understood in the context of the dynamics in countries and regions where the community-building process is advancing with intensity. As many more friends dedicate themselves to promoting the various activities to which the study of institute courses gives rise, distinct areas of learning associated with each of these activities steadily take shape in the life of a population. Some of these areas of learning, such as those concerned with collective worship, deepening, and teaching, are supported by Area Teaching Committees, while others related to the spiritual education of children, junior youth, and youth and adults are fostered by the training institutes. Additional areas of learning supported by other agencies also gradually come into place as more and more people study the higher courses of the institute's sequence. As the endeavours in each of these areas are sustained by growing numbers of friends, fresh insights are generated that are distinctive in that they arise from systematic effort undertaken in a particular social and cultural setting. There is an increasing understanding of what other concepts, approaches, abilities, and attitudes are essential to advancing an aspect of the community-building process. These become objects of conversation in periodic gatherings held to consult and reflect on the experience being gained. Aside from the initiatives individuals or institutions and agencies may take to respond to these needs, the institute might decide to promote the use of a supplementary material as described above. Over time, what is learned is captured by the institutions and agencies of the Faith in various documents, narrative accounts, and case studies which, in their totality, constitute a record of unfolding experience. When a sizeable body of knowledge accumulates, it becomes possible to further systematize it by developing a branch course.

We have in the past likened the main sequence to the trunk of a tree that supports other courses branching from it, each branch addressing some specific area of action. The preparation of such branch courses would necessarily occur over time through a pattern marked by action and reflection and in which conceptualization and activity in the field go hand in hand. For training institutes that take on this task, there are several requisites. They will need to be able to understand profoundly the content of the institute's main sequence and the pedagogical principles involved, analyse clearly the experience arising at the grassroots as activities advance, collaborate with teams of friends

7.7

dedicated to the progress of specific aspects of the community-building process, operate in a learning mode, and draw into their work individuals with abilities needed for preparing materials. Once in place, the branch course would help the friends promoting the related activity to further strengthen their capacity, and it would contribute to extending the associated process of learning in the life of the population. The course would also serve as a repository of the accruing knowledge and as a means for its propagation.

7.8   Developing materials of this nature is a complex exercise, and it is of course not a goal that every training institute develop its own branch courses. Training institutes, in consultation with the National Spiritual Assembly and the Counsellors, will determine when it is timely to develop or adopt such additional educational materials. Many institutes will simply select branch courses appropriate to their needs from those of proven effectiveness created by other institutes. Beyond branch courses, it is anticipated that institutes will in the future prepare or adopt other types of courses, which may be integrated in some way into the main sequence or be offered separately. This will, naturally, require the acquisition of even greater capacity by the institutes. However, notwithstanding the far-reaching effects of their efforts, institutes are not expected to address all the educational needs of the Bahá'í community. Within divers populations, large-scale growth will lead to new educational endeavours to address other pressing demands.

We are confident that, as the friends labour in all   7.9
regions to release the society-building power of the
Faith, the years ahead will witness a significant further
expansion of the capacity of training institutes to provide
spiritual education to large numbers and to generate,
apply, and disseminate knowledge. As part of its mandate
to watch over the process of human resource development, we have asked the International Teaching Centre
to follow closely the raising of capacity for preparing
educational materials. It will establish mechanisms
for supporting the institutes and for ensuring that
what is learned is appropriately propagated.

We will beseech the Blessed Beauty in the Holy   7.10
Shrines that the operations of training institutes,
these vital agencies of the Faith, may ever receive
His unfailing blessings and confirmations.

THE UNIVERSAL HOUSE OF JUSTICE

3 January 2022

To the Auxiliary Board members
throughout the world

Dearly loved Friends,

On this day that we had awaited with so much 8.1
anticipation to welcome you all in the Holy Land for a
joint conference with the members of the Continental
Boards of Counsellors, we feel moved to write to
you and express our sadness that, owing to world
conditions, this longed-for gathering could not
take place. The sentiments that we had hoped to
express to you in person must now be conveyed from
afar. But distance does not diminish the intensity of
the love we have for each one of you.

It is one hundred years to the day since the 8.2
first public reading of the Will and Testament of
'Abdu'l-Bahá. In that precious Document, He set out
the obligations of the Hands of the Cause of God, for
whose support the Auxiliary Boards for Propagation
and Protection were originally created. 'Abdu'l-Bahá
summoned the Hands of the Cause "to diffuse the
Divine Fragrances, to edify the souls of men, to
promote learning, to improve the character of all men
and to be, at all times and under all conditions,
sanctified and detached from earthly things." Reading
these words at this time evokes for us the service that

83

each of you are carrying out across the Bahá'í world. Indeed, the worldwide Bahá'í community owes a debt of gratitude to the entire institution of the Counsellors, including all those who have served as Continental Counsellors, Auxiliary Board members, and assistants in years gone by. Without such devoted service from so many, the marvellous advances made in recent decades, which are evident in the world today, could not have occurred. And an indispensable contribution to that progress has been the guidance and encouragement provided by the International Teaching Centre: an institution agile and perspicacious, and wholly indefatigable.

8.3   By now you have had the opportunity to become acquainted with the provisions of the Nine Year Plan and to ponder its implications. As will be apparent, the range of fields in which the believers are being asked to serve within their clusters, in order to release the society-building power of the Faith in ever-greater measures, has broadened. Correspondingly, the range of matters to which you must give serious attention has broadened as well. Your efforts are integral to the work of developing capacity to contribute to the Bahá'í community's various areas of endeavour, and your efforts are just as integral to helping the friends demonstrate in action the capacity they have acquired. In attending to both of these needs, and more generally in fulfilling your responsibilities for education and the improvement of character, you of course rely a great deal on the efficacy of the institute process. Ever since its creation, the institute has been an essential instrument for your work, and equally, your energetic support has been essential to its development. It brings us much joy, then, to see the pronounced, earnest spirit of collaboration that characterizes your relationship with all those responsible for coordinating the institute's endeavours.

You have no doubt read the description we 8.4 presented, in our message to the Counsellors a few days ago, of how you must help the friends to find a fitting response to each of the many challenges they encounter in their pursuit of the Plan. In this regard, we feel sure you are conscious that, however beneficial the influence of your counsel, the influence of your example will be greater still. A notable strength of your office is that it connects the believers with the different levels of Bahá'í administration and reinforces the spirit of cooperation that binds them together. You have a vital duty to help raise consciousness of the purpose of Bahá'í administration and to assist with the establishment and proper functioning of new Local Spiritual Assemblies. You keep the friends connected with the plans and projects of Bahá'í institutions operating at the local, regional, and national levels. Ultimately, you strengthen the connection between the friends and the Universal House of Justice by encouraging and leading the study of messages as they emerge. The believers look to you for a sound understanding of the Plan and for a courageous example of how to put its provisions into effect, especially in teaching the Faith. Your strong familiarity with the reality of circumstances in various clusters, combined with your thorough grasp of what is required for the Cause to advance, puts you in an ideal position to make thoughtful, creative, and timely contributions to consultations about how to release the society-building power of the Faith in every setting.

8.5   In addition to the foregoing, we wish to draw attention to your special role in encouraging the youth. So many youth who are now winning victories for the Cause were inspired by an Auxiliary Board member or assistant whose enthusiastic support and spirit of devotion taught them to rely on the power of divine confirmations and boldly enter the arena of service. Your responsibilities extend even further to the promotion of the education of children and junior youth, to the upliftment of the young, and to the strengthening of a pattern of family life that will produce generation after generation of consecrated souls, faithful followers of Bahá'u'lláh who have chosen the betterment of the world over the advancement of personal interests. The youth who, in the final year of the Nine Year Plan, will be carrying out acts of service to ensure its ultimate success are in many cases the children who, today, need to be nurtured in their love of the Blessed Beauty and their understanding of His mission.

8.6   Beloved friends, in your moments of prayer, be assured that all your entreaties to Bahá'u'lláh are accompanied by our own supplications in the Holy Shrines on your behalf. May your movement and your stillness be guided by the gentle winds of His Will, and may He bestow upon you the enduring bounty of being enabled to serve Him in accordance with His wish.

THE UNIVERSAL HOUSE OF JUSTICE

4 January 2022

To the Bahá'ís of the World

Dearly loved Friends,

We are at this moment with the company of the 9.1
Continental Counsellors—the great majority of them
present in the Holy Land, while some who could not
travel here join from a distance—and the sixth and
final day of their conference, focused on the upcoming
Nine Year Plan, is about to conclude. There is so much
that could be shared with you about the spirit of this
conference, as seen in its participants. Steeped in
experience, they have been eyewitnesses to the rise in
capacity in the Bahá'í world, and they brim with
confidence about what you can further accomplish.
We could not have wished for a keener, more insightful grasp of what is called for in the next Plan than was
demonstrated in the consultations of these consecrated
souls. But this, of course, is just the beginning. When
the Counsellors return to the countries of five
continents, they will bring to you and those who serve
with you all that they have absorbed. They and their
auxiliaries will be at your side as you prepare for this
immense collective enterprise—especially through
your participation in the wave of conferences soon to
sweep across the globe, where Bahá'u'lláh's universal
summons to work for the betterment of the world will
galvanize the assembled well-wishers of humanity.

9.2　　　A confluence of circumstances in the world at large and within the Faith has made this a charged moment. The global challenges now facing humanity are a severe test of its willingness to put aside short-term self-interest and come to terms with this stark spiritual and moral reality: there is but one, interconnected human family and it shares one precious homeland. At this same moment, the followers of Bahá'u'lláh are examining anew the possibilities before them to release the society-building power of the Faith. This Plan will test their stamina, their willpower, and the strength of their love for those who dwell alongside them. They will help to nurture, in every place, communities of common purpose that recognize the power of unity to heal, to transcend. Within these communities, every soul may find sanctuary, and in the friends' many endeavours for worship and praise, for education, for social transformation, for the development of communities—in all these, every soul may find room to grow and to serve. We are stirred by the promise of 'Abdu'l-Bahá: "The small shall be made great, and the powerless shall be given strength; they that are of tender age shall become the children of the Kingdom, and those that have gone astray shall be guided to their heavenly home."

9.3　　　When Bahá'u'lláh sent forth His glad tidings, the devoted believers who could carry His message to humanity were so few in number. Today, praise be to God, the devotion of the friends is undimmed and their numbers have soared. May their hearts be fortified through the power of His Word and, on every occasion and in every space, may they shine with the light of the splendours of heaven. Such will be the prayer on our tongues and the hope in our breasts when, today, with the Counsellors, we enter the Shrine of the Blessed Beauty to supplicate on your behalf.

THE UNIVERSAL HOUSE OF JUSTICE

Riḍván 2022

To the Bahá'ís of the World

Dearly loved Friends,

A year of preparation and reflection, as well as of great exertion, has concluded, distinguished by the efforts of the friends worldwide to mark the centenary of the Ascension of 'Abdu'l-Bahá, including by sending representatives to participate in a special event honouring Him in the Holy Land. Through these efforts, the inspiration offered by the life of 'Abdu'l-Bahá has been felt by countless souls and not only Bahá'ís. His concern for every member of the human family, His teaching work, His promotion of undertakings for education and social well-being, His profound contributions to discourses in both the East and the West, His heartfelt encouragement of projects to construct Houses of Worship, His shaping of early forms of Bahá'í administration, His cultivation of varied aspects of community life—all these complementary facets of His life were a reflection of His constant and complete dedication to serving God and serving humanity. Beyond being a towering figure of moral authority and surpassing spiritual insight, 'Abdu'l-Bahá was a pure channel through which the forces released by the Revelation of Bahá'u'lláh could act upon the world. To comprehend the society-building power possessed by the Faith, one need look no further

10.1

than the achievements of 'Abdu'l-Bahá during His ministry and the transformative effects of the guidance that flowed unceasingly from His pen. So many of the marvellous advances made by the present-day Bahá'í community—which were surveyed in our message to you last Riḍván—trace their origins to the actions, decisions, and directions of 'Abdu'l-Bahá.

10.2   How fitting, then, that the Bahá'í community's collective tribute to its perfect Exemplar should form the prelude to its commencement of a major undertaking focused on the release of the society-building power of the Faith in ever-greater measures. The areas of endeavour that fall within the scope of the Nine Year Plan, and of the current series of Plans, are directed towards the fulfilment of this overarching objective. It is also the focus of the more than 10,000 conferences being held across the globe to mark the launch of this great spiritual enterprise. These conferences, expected to welcome unprecedented numbers of participants, are bringing together not only Bahá'ís but many other well-wishers of humanity who share with them a longing to foster unity and better the world. Their determination and strong sense of purpose are reflected in the spirit generated at the gatherings that have already occurred, where the participants have been galvanized as much by the dynamic consultations to which they have contributed as by the collective vision explored at these joyful events. We look with eager anticipation to what the coming months and years will bring.

Since we addressed our 30 December 2021 10.3 message to the Counsellors' Conference, National Spiritual Assemblies and Regional Bahá'í Councils have been earnestly assessing the possibilities for intensifying the process of growth in the clusters within their jurisdiction during the Nine Year Plan. We feel it would be helpful, for the purpose of gauging the progress made over time, to view the Plan as unfolding in two phases of four and five years' duration, and National Assemblies were invited to consider the advances they expect to see in their respective communities by Riḍván 2026 and then by Riḍván 2031. This exercise also involved a re-evaluation of cluster boundaries, and the outcome of these adjustments is that the total number of clusters in the world has risen by a quarter and now stands at over 22,000. Judging by the forecasts received, it is estimated that, by the end of the Plan, a programme of growth at some level of development will exist in around 14,000 of these clusters. From among them, the number where the programme of growth could be considered intensive is projected to climb to 11,000 over the same time period. And of these, it is anticipated that the number of clusters where the third milestone has been passed will rise above 5,000 by 2031. Without question, to make such advances will entail colossal effort over the entire duration of the Plan. Yet we find these to be worthy aspirations towards which to strive, for they represent an ambitious but serious appraisal of what lies within reach.

10.4   This is telling. Such objectives could not be realistically contemplated if administrative institutions and agencies had not evolved markedly, endowing them with significantly heightened capacity to manage the affairs of a community whose activities have multiplied so quickly, embracing a vast and growing number of kindred souls. It would not be possible to aspire to such growth if a desire to learn—to act, to reflect, to capture insights, and to absorb the insights emerging elsewhere—had not been cultivated at all levels, extending to the grassroots of the community. And the effort implied by such projections would hardly be feasible if a systematic approach to the teaching work and to human resource development had not become increasingly manifest in the Bahá'í world. All this has brought about an advance in the Bahá'í community's awareness of its own identity and purpose. A determination to be outward looking in the process of community building had already become an established aspect of culture in many, many places; it has now blossomed, in a rising number of communities, into a sense of real responsibility for the spiritual and material progress of larger and larger groups within society, well beyond the membership of the Bahá'í community itself. The efforts of the friends to build communities, to engage in social action, and to contribute to the prevalent discourses of society have cohered into one global enterprise, bound together by a common framework for action, focused on helping humanity to establish its affairs on a foundation of spiritual principles. The significance of the developments we have described, reaching this point one hundred years after the inauguration of the Administrative Order, cannot be overlooked. In the extraordinary rise in capacity that has occurred in the last two decades—and which has made it possible for the Bahá'í world to view its endeavours in terms of the release of the society-building power of the Faith—we see incontrovertible evidence that the Cause of God has entered the sixth epoch of its Formative Age. We announced last Riḍván that the widespread phenomenon of large numbers participating in Bahá'í activities, being kindled by faith, and acquiring the skills and abilities to serve their communities signalled that the third epoch of the Master's Divine Plan had commenced; thus, the One Year Plan, at its inception then and at its conclusion now, has come to mark a set of historic advances made by the company of the faithful. And at the threshold of a new, mighty undertaking, this united body of believers stands ready to seize the possibilities wide open before it.

10.5   A prominent feature of the epoch that now ends was the erection of the last of the continental Houses of Worship and the initiation of projects to establish Houses of Worship at the national and local levels. Much has been learned, by Bahá'ís the world over, about the concept of the Mashriqu'l-Adhkár and the union of worship and service it embodies. During the sixth epoch of the Formative Age, much more will be learned about the path that leads from the development within a community of a flourishing devotional life—and the service which it inspires—to the appearance of a Mashriqu'l-Adhkár. Consultations are beginning with various National Spiritual Assemblies, and as these proceed, we will periodically announce places where a Bahá'í House of Worship will be raised up in the coming years.

10.6   Our joy at seeing the community of the Greatest Name go from strength to strength is tempered by our deep sorrow at seeing the persistence of conditions and conflicts in the world that create misery and desperate suffering—in particular, at observing the recrudescence of destructive forces that have disordered international affairs while visiting horrors upon populations. We know well and are reassured that, as Bahá'í communities have repeatedly demonstrated in many different contexts, the followers of Bahá'u'lláh are committed to offering relief and support to those around them, no matter how straitened their own circumstances. But until humanity as a whole undertakes to establish its affairs on foundations of justice and truth, it is, alas, fated to stagger from one crisis to another. We pray that, if the recent outbreak of war in Europe is to yield any lessons for the future, it will serve as an urgent reminder of the course that the world must take if it is to attain genuine and enduring peace. The principles enunciated by Bahá'u'lláh to the monarchs and presidents of His time, and the weighty responsibilities with which He charged rulers past and present, are perhaps even more pertinent and imperative today than when they were first recorded by His Pen. For Bahá'ís, the inexorable advance of the Major Plan of God—bringing with it ordeals and upheavals, but ultimately impelling humanity towards justice, peace, and unity—is the context within which the Minor Plan of God, with which the believers are chiefly occupied, unfolds. The dysfunctional state of present-day society makes the need for the release of the society-building power of the Faith abundantly clear and pressing. We cannot but expect that, for now, convulsions and disturbances will continue to afflict the world; you will no doubt appreciate, then, why every earnest supplication we offer for all God's children to be relieved from bewilderment and bitter hardship is coupled with an equally heartfelt prayer for the success of the much-needed service you are rendering for the Cause of the Prince of Peace.

In every cluster where the activities of the Plan 10.7 are gaining momentum, we see the development of communities with the noble characteristics we described in the 30 December 2021 message. As societies experience stresses of various kinds, the followers of the Abhá Beauty must stand out more and more for their qualities of resilience and rationality, for their standard of conduct and their adherence to principle, and for the compassion, detachment, and forbearance they demonstrate in their pursuit of unity. Time and again, the distinctive characteristics and attitudes shown by the believers in periods of acute difficulty have prompted people to turn to Bahá'ís for explanation, counsel, and support, especially when the life of a society has been upset by peril and unforeseen disruptions. In sharing these observations, we are mindful that the Bahá'í community itself also experiences the effects of the forces of disintegration at work in the world. Moreover, we are conscious that the greater the friends' efforts to promote the Word of God, the stronger the countervailing forces they will encounter, sooner or later, from various quarters. They must fortify their minds and spirits against the tests that are sure to come, lest these impair the integrity of their endeavours. But the believers know well that whatever storms lie ahead, the ark of the Cause is equal to them all. Successive stages of its voyage have seen it weather the elements and ride the waves. Now it is bound for a new horizon. The confirmations of the Almighty are the gusts that fill its sails and propel it towards its destination. And the Covenant is its lodestar, keeping the sacred vessel set on its sure and certain course. May the hosts of heaven send blessings upon all who sail within.

THE UNIVERSAL HOUSE OF JUSTICE

NOTES